THE MISSIONARY IDEAL IN THE SCOTTISH CHURCHES

*This gospel of the kingdom shall
be preached in all the world for a
witness unto all nations ; and then shall
the end come (Matt. XXIV, 14.)*

The Missionary Ideal in the Scottish Churches

The Chalmers' Lectures delivered in 1926 by the Rev. D. Mackichan, D.D., LL.D., F.R.S.E., Hon. Principal, Wilson College, Bombay; and some-time Vice-Chancellor of the University, Bombay.

Hodder and Stoughton
Publishers   London

Made and Printed in Great Britain for Hodder & Stoughton, Limited,
by C. Tinling & Co., Ltd., Liverpool, London and Prescot.

CONTENTS

PREFATORY NOTE

IN these days when " of making many books there is no end," it is generally felt by those who venture to add to their number to be necessary to justify their action.

The Trustees of the Chalmers' Lectureship have absolved me from this necessity by ordaining that the lectures delivered on this foundation shall be published in the year following that of their delivery.

This volume contains in substance the lectures as they were originally prepared for delivery in 1926. In the actual delivery, some abridgement was, of course, necessary in order to keep the time of delivery within reasonable limits.

While in publishing these lectures I am simply complying with the conditions of the lectureship, I still venture to hope that their publication may not be inopportune at the present period in missionary history when it is so essential that the Church should realize its supreme duty and discern its great opportunity.

D. MACKICHAN.

EDINBURGH,
   31st May, 1927.

In the lectures which have hitherto been delivered under the Chalmers' Foundation, in accordance with the purpose of the founder of the lectureship, the Scottish Churches have been presented in various aspects of their life and work. Lecturers have discussed their origin, their constitution, their relation to the peculiar genius of the Scottish nation and also their expansion, following the migrations of the Scottish people, into the remotest parts of the Empire. Not only the ecclesiastical organization developed within these Churches, but also the forms of public worship in which the religion of the Scottish people expressed itself, have furnished a succession of Chalmers' lecturers with appropriate subjects.

When the present writer, on his appointment to this lectureship, addressed himself to the selection of a suitable subject he found that one side of the work of the Scottish

Churches, and in his view the most important, had been omitted in the lectures hitherto delivered, viz., the part which they had played in the wider mission of the Church to the world. He accordingly resolved to select as the subject of this course " The Scottish Churches and the Missionary Ideal." The choice of this subject seemed to be demanded by the special circumstances of the times in which we are living.

One of the most important among the changes which have resulted from the recent convulsion that has shaken so many of the nations is the emergence of a new vision of the world and of our national and personal responsibilities in relation to it. The horizon of most nations has been vastly widened and, while in every land the national consciousness has been intensified, a keener sense also of international obligation has taken possession of many minds, most of all, of the Christian mind. This idea of the world-wide obligations of the Church of Christ is imbedded in the foundations of our faith ; but in the earliest days of the Christian Church it did not emerge into thought and action till the struggle with the particularism of the nation in which Christianity had its first home obtained its earliest victory. It was the Christian fact that " to the Gentiles also hath God granted repentance unto life " that launched the Church on its universal mission, and in all the subsequent ages of its history the convincing power of accomplished fact has been needed to keep alive or re-awaken a consciousness that tended to slumber. From age to age God moved chosen spirits to the great Christian adventure and the facts of missionary achievement continued to preserve within the Church some sense of a world-responsibility.

Amongst other causes lying outside the Church's own special sphere which contributed to this result was the advance of geographical discovery, an increasing knowledge of the races of mankind, and, in addition to this, great world movements that changed their history.

It is more than a mere coincidence that the closing years of the 18th and the opening years of the 19th century, when the tread of great armies resounded throughout Europe and this land of ours was overshadowed by the fear of a Napoleonic invasion, were marked by a great spiritual renaissance that gave birth to the missionary movement of the modern age. It seems as if " the removing of those things that are shaken as of things that are made " threw men back on the things that cannot be shaken. The eternal realities took possession anew of the hearts of multitudes amid the crash of the things that are temporal. Many responded to the new call to consecration and service, and the life of an awakened Church began to pour itself forth in new efforts to make known to those who had so long sat in darkness a Gospel which had begun to shed new light on their own land.

How many celebrations of the centenary of the foundation of great Christian philanthropic and missionary societies have we not witnessed in our own time ? Will our successors a hundred years hence be similarly occupied in celebrating the centenary of like movements initiated in the eventful years through which the world is now passing ? The opening years of this century have been full of unprecedented happenings. Scenes of horror, of suffering and sacrifice have been witnessed, before which those of a century ago pale into utter insignificance. We have seen one side of the picture ; are we to see the other also ? Are we to see in our day, as our forefathers saw in theirs, the beginnings of a renaissance of Christian faith bringing a new consciousness of our missionary responsibility towards those nations to which Christ's message has not yet been brought ? We are perhaps too near the events which have awakened this expectancy to measure the possibilities which they contain ; the re-action which always seems to follow upon a period of strain and exhausting anguish is not yet past. Yet the signs of the coming of a new era in missionary endeavour are not wanting. Amongst these we reckon the new attitude which is discernible in all the Churches, and also outside the Churches, towards the missionary activity of our time. A century ago it was necessary, even within the Church, to defend the cause of Missions. Such defence is no longer called for : the missionary ideal now holds an undisputed place within the general scheme of the Church's life. Whether it has yet gained its rightful place amid its practical activities is another question ; but the conviction has now come to many that the establishment of the rule of Christ among all nations is the supreme end of the Church which He founded in the world.

Some of us can remember the time when this conception of the missionary ideal began to dawn upon the mind of the Scottish Churches. The vision has grown. How far it has advanced to true realization it will be our endeavour in succeeding chapters to expound. There has never indeed been a time in the period over which the memory of any of us extends when it was not recognized in our Scottish Churches that without its Foreign Mission no Church could be held to be fulfilling its highest purpose. Still the point of view from which they regarded their missionary responsibility was not that which we have above indicated. In their view the Foreign Mission was a necessary supplement to all the other activities, something essential for a complete well-rounded Church-life. To dislodge this conception of the missionary ideal, to raise it from this secondary to its primal place is a task of stupendous difficulty ; but this is the task which the Church must resolutely face to-day. The day must come when it will be recognized throughout the Churches that no professing Christian, who does not share in some degree the passion of his Lord for the salvation of men of all kindreds and tongues and nations, has realized his place in the kingdom of God.

We shall see as we proceed that this view of the Christian life and its missionary obligation is demanded not only for the sake of the world but also for the true well-being of the Church itself.

And most fittingly do we link this study with the great name of Chalmers who from out the din and the dust of ecclesiastical conflict seemed with those wistful eyes of his to be ever gazing towards a wider horizon than that which bounded the vision of so many of his day. Already we seem to be within sight of the realization of one of his visions, that of a Scottish Church equipped and organized to minister to the spiritual needs of the Scottish nation. The fulfilment of that other vision which touched his great soul to a still higher expectancy, while still distant, is drawing ever nearer.

" We were now treading that illustrious island (Icolmkill) which was once the luminary of the Caledonian regions, whence savage clans and roving barbarians derived the benefits of knowledge and the blessings of religion. . . . Far from me and my friends be such frigid philosophy as may conduct us indifferent and unmoved over any ground which has been dignified by wisdom or virtue. That man is little to be envied whose patriotism would not gain force upon the plain of Marathon or whose piety would not grow warmer among the ruins of Iona."

SAMUEL JOHNSON,
Tour of the Western Isles.

The name of the Scottish people, of their country and their Church, proclaims their affinity with that branch of the Keltic race which in the course of its westward migration found a home in the sister isle of Ireland. The race which then settled in Ireland was known in the early centuries of the Christian era as the " Scoti." In Adamnan's *Life of S. Columba,* " Scotia " is the standing designation of Ireland, and in the *Hist. Eccl.* of the Venerable Bede, " Scotia " has the same application. In view of those features of character which are supposed to belong to the typical Scot of to-day, the familiar expression *praefervidum ingenium Scotorum* may have sometimes sounded not a little incongruous. The *praefervidum ingenium*, the fiery temperament, is scarcely a distinctive possession of the modern Scot into whose composition other racial elements have entered ; but it is conspicuous to-day in the Irish people regarding whom the expression was in the first instance used, and also in those Keltic sections of the Scottish people who for many generations held aloof in language and in culture from the other inhabitants of Scotland. This Keltic section, a small minority of the Scottish nation, have given their name to the entire country and the mingling of their blood with that of races of different type has made the Scottish people what they are, for good or for evil.

It has been very truly remarked that Scotland has no history apart from the history of the Scottish Church, and the explanation of the singular phenomenon

B

now alluded to in connection with the naming of the nation is simply this, that the earliest form of Christianity that obtained a really permanent hold on the life of Scotland came to it from the Keltic missionary Church of the Ireland of the Scots.

A brief incursion into the field of the history of the first planting of the Christian religion in the British Isles will enable us to recognize the significance for our present subject of the manner of the entrance of Christianity into these islands. Only the chief landmarks in this history require to be noted.

The impact of Irish Christianity on Scotland was not the earliest instance of Scotland's contact with the new faith ; but it was the most permanent in its results, continuing as it did to extend the sphere of its influence and to nourish the Christian life of Scotland from generation to generation through the early centuries.

The Roman occupation of Britain which continued up to the year 410 of the Christian era opened up our island to Continental influence and prepared the way for the advent of the Christian religion to Britain. The channels through which it entered must remain unknown. It has been conjectured with some probability that traders from Gaul and other parts of the Roman Empire, following in the wake of the Roman legions, had made converts to the new faith from among the ancient Britons, who represented a stream of Keltic migration from the East akin to that which entered Ireland ; for according to the testimony of Tertullian and Origen, given in the opening years of the 3rd century, Christianity had gained a foothold in these islands before the close of the 2nd century. Church history records that in the 4th century the Church which had grown out of these early beginnings was represented in the Church Council which met at Arles by a bishop, priest and deacon. And not long after it attained the distinction of producing a famous heretic, Pelagius the Briton, who found his way to Rome, the centre of the Christian Church in that age.

The influence of this early British Christianity, which, it should be noted, stood in intimate relation to the Roman See, did not penetrate, except fitfully, to the northern

parts of Britain. Scotland (using now the
name in its modern application) received no
extensive or permanent influence from this
source. St. Ninian (Ringan) a Christian of
the British race, after visiting Rome and
Tours where he came under the strong
influence of St. Martin, on his return to his
own country pushed northwards to the
Galloway peninsula and founded in the Isle
of Whithorn a church, the famous *Candida
Casa*, which he dedicated to St. Martin. His
activities lay among the Picts, some of this
race having established themselves in the
South of Scotland. His personal missionary
activity was, in all probability, confined
within these limits. In the north-eastern
parts of Scotland there are a number of
dedications which bear the name of the
saint ; but these are not accepted by some
of the best authorities as an evidence of St.
Ninian's actual presence and personal labours
in those remoter regions, the honour in which
this saint was held by those of his followers
who laboured in those parts being a sufficient
explanation of the origin of the name they
bear. When the Britons were conquered by
the invading heathen hosts of Jutes, Saxons

and Angles the British Church vanished from the conquered territories which relapsed into paganism. Those who remained faithful to the Christian religion retired to the Western districts. St. Ninian's influence lingered for some time in his own settlement in Galloway, but for little more than a hundred years.

Similarly shortlived were the immediate fruits of the labours of another of the Britons, Kentigern, better known as St. Mungo, who settled at the beginning of the 6th century on the banks of the Molendinar, a small tributary of the Clyde, and there founded a settlement out of which some centuries later grew the See of Glasgow. St. Mungo, after a compulsory retreat to Wales, returned to his Scottish seat and re-established himself there, but for four centuries he had no successor.

These two tides of evangelization proceeding from the British Church, which suffered such a speedy arrest, having proved so temporary in their direct result, we must look elsewhere for the origin of the movement which led to the firm planting of the Christian Church in Scotland.

For the accomplishment of this task, one who was a contemporary of St. Mungo was being prepared within the bosom of the Irish Church—Columba, who stands out [1] pre-eminent as the evangelizer of Scotland.

The beginnings of the Church in Ireland, from which this missionary sprang are hid in obscurity. The earliest Christian influence which reached Ireland is supposed to have come through Gallic traders in the 3rd century. Before the end of the 4th century Ireland, too, had produced its heretic in the person of Celestius, an adherent of Pelagius the Briton.

The history of the Irish Church emerges into clearer light with two names which represent real personalities, Palladius and Patricius. The mission of Palladius, sent as a bishop to Ireland by Pope Celestinus, is generally regarded as historical; but so little is known regarding it that the best authorities have concluded that it must have

---

[1] Recent investigations into the origins of Christianity amongst the Picts of Northern Scotland, while interesting and important as contributions to early Church history, do not invalidate the claim of Columba's name to the place of pre-eminence which it has so long held in the history of Scottish Christianity.

been of short duration and that it ended in failure, perhaps in martyrdom.

On the other hand in the case of Patricius we have two documents which have been accepted by the most competent authorities as genuine, the *Confessio Patricii* and the *Epistola Patricii*. From these two sources a detailed record of his life and his mission to Ireland is obtained.[1]

St. Patrick's "Confession" is really an auto-

---

[1] The *Epistola ad Coroticum* adds little in the way of direct information regarding the life of St. Patrick ; but it is of interest and importance in determining the question of the date and genuineness both of the *Confessio* and the *Epistola*. The *Epistola* is addressed to a certain Coroticus, a leader whose plundering followers had made a raid upon Irish Christians, including men and women of high birth, a number of whom they had deported and sold into slavery in distant countries. In this open letter addressed to Coroticus the writer remonstrates with the offenders and calls upon them to return the captives, dwelling on the enormity of their guilt and the punishment at the hand of God which awaits such evil-doers. He refers to the prevalence of such crimes and reminds Coroticus how the Churches of Rome and Gaul had been constrained to send messengers with large sums of money to the Franks in order to ransom Christians thus abducted and sold into slavery The writer speaks of the many thousands he had brought into the Christian Church. In order apparently to give weight to his remonstrance he refers to his own noble birth and to his father's official position. Little doubt is thus left as to the authorship of the two writings ascribed to Patricius, and the allusion to the experiences of the Gallic and Roman churches, as well as the Scripture quotations, go far to enable the date of these writings, and inferentially that of St. Patrick, to be determined.

biography in which the author, in daily danger of death or imprisonment, seeks to bear witness to the unmerited grace of the triune God who had taken him as " a stone out of the mire " and " set him on a lofty wall to bear his testimony before great and small." This " Confession " he bequeaths as his legacy to his brethren in Gaul and to his sons in the Lord of whom he had baptized many thousands.

Patricius, according to his own narrative, was born of Christian parents, being the son of a presbyter who lived in Bennavem [1] of Tabernia. He was of gentle birth, his father being a " decurio " or magistrate of a provincial town in Britain.

Along with many others Patricius was taken captive in an Irish raid on the coasts

---

[1] The identification of the place of St. Patrick's birth has long been the subject of inquiry and debate. His birthplace has been claimed for Scotland and identified with a village on the banks of the Clyde which bears the name of " Kilpatrick," a name which embodies this tradition and is the result of it. This old and long accepted tradition has, however, been questioned. The Rev. Dr. Hewison of Rothesay has been one of the more recent opponents of this tradition and has written learnedly in support of a different identification which places the birthplace of the saint somewhere in the region of the Solway coast, where a number of dedications in the name of St. Patrick have been discovered.

of Britain and brought to Hibernia (Ireland), where he remained in slavery for six years serving as a shepherd. He escaped from Ireland in a ship the sailors of which were pagans, and after voyaging for three days reached land, probably the coast of Gaul. There, after wandering for twenty-eight days through a desert region, he was again taken captive. After two months he was delivered from the hands of his captors and made his escape to the Mediterranean coast, from which a few years later he found his way back to his parents in Britain.

In consequence of a vision, in which he heard the cry of the Irish, " We beseech thee, holy youth, to come hither and work among us," he resolved to leave his country and kindred and to go to Ireland as a missionary. He received ordination as a deacon, then as a presbyter, and ultimately in his forty-fifth year as a bishop. He would seem to have gone to Ireland while still a presbyter. His work during the remaining years of his life was that of an ardent evangelist. Possessed of a minute knowledge of the Bible he carried his message with artless and pathetic eloquence and often amid great personal danger throughout the land from the year A.D. 432 till his death in the year 461.

There were then no episcopal dioceses in the land ; the early Christian Irish Scots were not in subjection to the Roman See. Nor were they, in the modern sense, ecclesiastically organized. Their religious life was centred around monastic settlements from which an evangelical influence radiated out into the surrounding districts. Ireland was still under the tribal system and the progress of Christianity followed lines which were marked out for it by the prevailing social order. The missionaries were wont to address themselves in the first instance to the winning of the chief or ruler of the tribe ; the monastery was generally established in some strong place, granted by him on his conversion to the faith, and working from this centre the missionaries gradually succeeded in bringing the people of the tribe under the influence of Christian teaching and Christian life.

The monastic order as it shaped itself in Ireland was not regulated by the Church system. At the head of the monastery stood the Abbot whose ordination might be that of a simple presbyter, while the members under his rule might, not unfrequently, include men who had been ordained as bishops of the Church.

From the point of view of Rome this was quite an anomalous constitution ; it sprang out of the missionary character of the Church in Ireland. For these monasteries, it must be remembered, were very different in their origin and purpose from the monasteries that originated in the East, to which they bore a resemblance that was mainly external. They did not spring from the ascetic motive as did those of the East ; nor were they places of refuge for the quietist Christian from a sinful and corrupt world, contact with which was regarded as an impediment to the attainment of the highest spiritual life. They were simply Mission stations through which a life-giving contact might be established with a people that sat in darkness. There was a beautiful and natural simplicity in the life that was lived in these early missionary settlements, the nearest counterpart to which is seen to-day in the Mission field in heathen lands or in Christian " settlements " in the darkest parts of a modern city at home.

The bishop who joined such a monastery

came not to rule over the brethren in the
monastic community ; he was content to
serve. The abbot who ruled was generally
the founder of the settlement and exercised
authority not in virtue of ecclesiastical rank,
but on the ground of evangelistic zeal and
enterprise.

The resemblance between those Keltic
foundations and the modern Mission station
is specially striking in the case of those
Mission fields in which the people stand on a
plane of civilization not far removed from that
occupied by the tribes for whose evangelization those monastic institutions were established. In Africa we see many illustrations
of this ancient method. The missionary
addresses his efforts to the tribe as well as to
the individual. The work of the Mission is
a civilizing as well as an evangelizing agency.
The Missions of the Scottish Churches in
Calabar, Livingstonia, Blantyre and Kaffraria
and to the depressed classes in India are to-day
following the lines along which the Irish and
the Alban Scots were themselves first guided
into the Church of Christ. These Missions
are working from centres of industrial and
educational as well as religious life.   For the

acceptance of the Christian faith means not merely the substitution of new beliefs for the old superstitions, but also a change in the social life of the community, a new attitude towards industry, the substitution of civilized for the more primitive methods of supporting life and of regulating the relations of men to one another.

The monastic type which those ancient Missions adopted was due also to the fact that they owed their origin to the spontaneous efforts of consecrated men. They did not spring out of the organized Church life ; they were born of the high spiritual enthusiasm of individual leaders, men who had heard the voice of God within their own souls and had listened to the cry that came to them from the need of the world.

There was at this time a great organized Church in the world which was already assuming for itself a place among the king-doms of the earth, already entering on the downward path that led to the assumption of temporal power. Already the Church had begun to be regarded as an end in itself. But those early apostles of the Keltic Church had sprung from a section of Christendom

which was only remotely touched by the
influence of the Central Roman Church.
There was, now that the Roman occupation
of Britain had ended, no contact, except in a
few isolated individual cases, of the Keltic
Irish Church with the Mother city. In its
remoteness and isolation it was free to
realize ideals which had been inherited from
an earlier age of apostolic simplicity. It was
and remained a Missionary Church with the
evangelization of the pagan population around
it as its pre-eminent function.

The history of the Keltic Church has often
been studied in a controversial spirit and
been exploited in the interests of a particular
form of Church government. This seems a
rather trivial use to make of the history of
this ancient Church. It did not consciously
stand for any particular theory of Church
government. The lesson which it teaches is
rather that external organization is of
secondary importance and is subordinate to
the Church's paramount aim, the spreading of
the kingdom of God. It had bishops among
the members of its monasteries, but it took
no account of ecclesiastical rank in the
organization of those monasteries. Spiritual

fitness to initiate or guide a religious movement was the primary qualification for leadership; the multiplication of centres of evangelism and not the consolidation of the organized Church was its objective. It was in possession of an evangel that was purer than that of the contemporary Roman Church, because it drew its traditions from a higher point in the stream than that at which the Church in Rome, already advanced in degeneration, now stood. But while this is true and full of significance, we cannot claim for it immunity from errors and corruptions that had crept into the ancient Church in those earlier periods of its history. The place which it gave to the sacraments, the efficacy which it ascribed to outward rites, would scarcely find acceptance in the evangelical Churches of to-day. Those things it simply took for granted, as it did also the orders of bishops, presbyters and deacons, without any definite theory held or taught regarding them.

In many points, however, this ancient Church shewed a marked divergence from Roman usage, for example, in regard to the law of celibacy for the clergy, the mode of tonsure, and the method of determinating the date of Easter. The reason of this divergence has been already indicated. This Church in its isolation remained long immune from Roman influence. Its traditions came to it from a comparatively early stage in the history of the Christian faith, and it had no knowledge of the later Church Councils and their decrees. Centuries were to elapse before this Church became fully absorbed by Rome and assimilated to it in discipline and practice. It had thus a simpler and a purer Gospel to proclaim and its message, reinforced by the loving ministry of devoted apostolic men, not only diffused a vigorous Christianity throughout Ireland but also accomplished a marvellous work in winning Scotland from paganism when it sent its missionaries to our shores.

The outstanding name in connection with this expansion of this Keltic Scottish Church into our country, to which it gave its name, is that of Columba, Colum-cille (the dove of the Church), whose birth has been assigned to the year 521 A.D. Of royal birth on both his father's and his mother's side he manifested from his early years a religious bent and was sent for his religious training to two great monastic centres in his native country, Moville and Clonard.[1]

When Columba emerged from the stage of preparation he immediately threw himself with conspicuous zeal and energy into the sacred task to which he had devoted his life, that of spreading the Gospel amongst his pagan countrymen. His abundant labours appear to have been most fruitful. Following

[1] To this period probably belongs the familiar story of Columba's controversy with Finnian, Abbot of Clonard, regarding the possession of a transcript of the Latin Psalter made by Columba from a copy lent him by the Abbot. One of Columba's favourite occupations was the copying of manuscripts, an art in which the Irish monks attained a very high excellence. One of the last duties in which he was engaged a few hours before his death was the transcribing of a MS. of the *Book of Psalms*, the completion of which was arrested by the failure of his strength. The story of his controversy with Finnian is thus described in the ancient Keltic record : " Finnian said that it was to himself belonged the son-book (copy) which was written from his book, and they both selected Diarmid (son of King Fergus) as judge between them. This is the decision that Diarmid made : that to every book belongs its son-book (copy) as to every cow belongs her calf."

This book, with its silver case, forms the ancient reliquary called the *Cathach* (praeliator, warrior). For generations the O'Donnells had this reliquary in their possession. It received its name from the tradition regarding it, viz., that if it were sent right-wise around the army it ensured victory in battle. It was also ordained that the casket should never be opened. The *cathach* now resides in the Museum of the Royal Irish Academy in Dublin, to which it was generously gifted by its owner.

Before it passed into the custody of the Museum it had been the subject of an interesting episode. A number of years ago a legal question as to some titles arose on which it was thought the armorial bearings on the silver shrine might possibly throw some light. The precious shrine was accordingly sent to a

C

the established method he founded numerous monasteries. Tradition gives the number of his foundations as 300 ; but the famous monasteries in Ireland which indubitably were due to his evangelistic labours would be sufficient of themselves as a testimony to the depth and the extent of his influence.

The year 563 marks a great crisis in his career ; for in his forty-second year he passed over to Scotland on a still wider and, in its

Dublin expert, who, before he could be entrusted with the casket, had to give a solemn undertaking that he would not attempt to open it. This prohibition seems only to have had the effect of whetting his curiosity. Finding a small hole in the casket he inserted a wire the movements of which within the casket were accompanied by the sound of rustling leaves. He then, unable longer to restrain his curiosity, opened the casket and found within a decayed wooden box enclosed in the silver shrine 55 sheets of MS. Some of the leaves had been destroyed through the rotting of the wood ; but those which had remained intact were found to be a transcript of the greater part of the Latin Psalter differing, however, in some places from the Vulgate. The caligraphy was held by some experts to be similar to that seen in MSS. belonging to the age of Columba. Experts generally differ in regard to problems of this nature ; but against the adverse opinion of some authorities the claim made on behalf of this ancient MS. that it is in the handwriting of Columba derives weight from the peculiar veneration in which it was so long held in past ages notwithstanding the total absence of decoration. If this identification be correct this may very probably be the very copy regarding the possession of which Columba had his dispute with the venerable abbot.

The sequel of this discovery is interesting. The indignant O'Donnells had the expert who, in breach of a solemn undertaking, had opened the casket, arraigned before the Dublin Court charged with the violation of his undertaking. The Chief Justice, however, assoilzied the accused on the ground that the silver casket had not been opened with any malicious intent.

ultimate results, greater and more fruitful mission.

A persistent tradition connects Columba's mission to Scotland with the sanguinary battle of Culdrehmne. The tradition bears that Columba, on account of the part which he had played in the bringing on of this conflict in which, it is said, 3,000 of Columba's fellow-countrymen perished, was excommunicated and banished from Ireland, and was forbidden to settle in any place from which the Irish coast could be descried. If we accepted this tale as it stands we should have to regard the great saint as a missionary by compulsion or accident, and not a heaven-sent ambassador moved by a great evangelic passion to win pagan Scotland to the faith of Christ.

The bloody conflict referred to took place between the northern and southern branches of the Hy-neill race. Columba was related by kinship to the northern section, while Diarmid was king of the southern section. In some minor feud between the two sections Diarmid is said to have slain one of his enemies who had sought the protection of Columba. From this incident or some similar occurrence sprang the war between north and south which culminated in this fierce battle. Columba was supposed to have encouraged or incited his kinsmen to enter on this conflict and was, therefore, visited with excommunication and sentenced to banishment.

This tradition is found in records which belong to a somewhat later age than that of Columba, and while we may accept it so far as it connects his name with the inter-tribal feud which resulted in the tragedy of a battle which so deeply impressed itself on the mind of the nation, there are the strongest possible reasons for refusing to accept the ingenious theory as to the origin of Columba's mission which it built upon this foundation. It is quite conceivable that Columba, stirred to indignation by a flagrant violation of the rights of sanctuary, may have moved his people to vindicate these rights in the spirit and according to the methods of that age, and it is not improbable that the Church in Ireland felt impelled by the terrible bloodshed which had been witnessed to express its disapproval of Columba's connection with it ; but we look in vain for any indication in the subsequent relations of the Church to Columba of the existence of the ban which it was said to have pronounced upon him. When, for example, he came on one occasion to a meeting of the Synod which is said to have excommunicated him, St. Brendan, we are told, rose and kissed him saying that " he was fore-ordained of God to be the leader of his people to life." His repeated visits to the home-church after he had laboured in Iona and throughout Scotland are scarcely reconcilable with the supposition that the stigma of excommunication had ever rested upon him.

There was also current in those old days another theory of Columba's dedication to the work of a missionary to another land. Columba is described as having been touched to deepest penitence for the part which he had played in this transaction, and that the penance prescribed was that he should go forth to save from death as many souls as he had caused to perish in the fateful conflict at Culdrehmne.

We may safely dismiss these explanations of the origin of Columba's mission. The record of his early life, his surrender of the worldly prospects which his birth and position opened to him, for the sake of a religious calling, his devoted labours through many years in his own country and the still more remarkable achievements of his mission to Scotland with its revelation of that tender love and Christ-like humility which won for him the highest place in the order of Scottish sainthood, will not fit into the somewhat artificially constructed story of an excommunicated and discredited ecclesiastic banished by his brethren and transformed *perforce* into a missionary to our pagan forefathers in Scotland.

Columba's mission to Scotland was not due to any accident, it was not forced upon him by any external necessity but by that inward necessity which has been the missionary motive of all the Christian centuries. This motive was deeply imbedded in the life of the Church to which he belonged, a Church which was yet to give proof of the wideness of its vision by sending forth its missionaries to much more distant fields. From this Church went forth many others, moved by the same evangelistic zeal which sent Columba to Scotland, trained like him in Irish monasteries,

to missionary service on the continent of
Europe, men like Columbanus and his com-
panions who brought their message to France,
Germany, Switzerland, and ultimately to
Italy. At the period to which these events
belong the Irish Keltic Church stood out as
the chief centre both of intellectual and
spiritual culture in Western Europe. The
ingenium Scotorum was not only perfervid ;
it was also luminous. From this remote
corner of Christendom, inhabited by the Scots,
radiated influences that tended not only
to the spread of Christianity but also to a
wide diffusion of learning. Down through
mediæval times it maintained this character,
and the appellation *Scotus* appears more
than once among the names found in the roll
of the more eminent Schoolmen. No section
of the Christian Church had a wider outlook
in that early age ; and, when we consider the
outstanding characteristics of the Scottish
nation to-day and the place which the
Churches of their little country occupy in the
ever-widening field of missionary enterprise,
it is difficult to resist the conviction that the
impress which the ancient Church of the
Keltic Scots left upon the national life of

Scotland has not been entirely effaced by the centuries that have passed since Columba the Scot first touched its shores.

The year 563 A.D. has been generally accepted as the date of Columba's crossing from Ireland to Scotland. He was then in his forty-second year. He chose for his settlement the little island which we now know as Iona, separated by a narrow strait from the south-western corner of the island of Mull. Its ancient name was *Hy* which appears in numerous variants as *Hi*, *Hii*, *Ia*, or simply *I*. The present name *Iona* is said to be due to a misreading of the text of Adamnan, Columba's biographer, whose habit of using adjectival forms led him to call Columba's isle *Ioua insula;* the letter " u " having been confounded with " n " the name Iona was the result. This name commended itself further by its similarity to the Hebrew יוֹנָה (dove), thus reproducing the name of Iona's saint, " the dove of the Church."

Long before the arrival of Columba there were already in Alban Scotland colonies of Scots from Ireland, a large proportion of whom were, at least nominally, Christian ; but the Picts were pagans. It was the

conversion of this pagan Pictish population
that was the principal objective of Columba's
mission. The peninsula of Kintyre, large
adjacent tracts of country and many islands
occupied by a body of colonists from Dalriada
in Ireland, had been formed into a kingdom
under the same name and were, when Columba
arrived on his mission, under the rule of king
Connal to whom Columba was related. This
Keltic king made to him a grant of the island
of Iona, which was within his territories ; in
this following the precedent set by the early
Irish kings or tribal chiefs who on their
conversion to Christianity made similar grants
of territory to monastic settlements.

In this island Columba established his
monastery and from this centre all his future
activities proceeded. It was conveniently situated for his purpose, standing near the border
line between the Scots and the Picts who
occupied mainly the tracts lying to the north.
We are left to glean from his biographers the
scanty information which they supply
regarding the manner in which he spread the
knowledge of the Gospel amongst the heathen
population of the land. The art of biography
is one of the most difficult among literary

arts. Even to-day how few seem to have attained a high proficiency in it ! Columba's biographers, of whom Adamnan is the chief, are sadly disappointing to the reader who is eager to know how the gospel made its way amongst the people. We would give much for a simple narrative of what this apostle did in presenting his message to a heathen tribe. Ancient records tell us of the numerous monasteries which he founded, but very little of his evangelistic methods. We can gather from these records that he followed the traditions which he brought with him from his native land. The social institutions of the various countries in which Christianity was planted in the early centuries had an important influence on the methods adopted by the first missionaries to those lands. From the information that has been handed down to us of the manner in which Christianity displaced paganism in Ireland and Scotland we can see that the tribal system played a very important part. We read so often of efforts made to win, in the first instance, the head of a tribe and of the members of the clan subsequently following their chief into the Christian fold and forming themselves into a Christian community with the monastery as its centre. In the modern Mission also in the case of tribes living under similar rule we meet with parallels to those ancient methods. Columba's greatest achievement along this line was the conversion of the Picts in the North who were under the wide dominion of Brude the Pictish king. Once this king was won to the faith his people followed. It was what we now describe as a mass-movement. In India to-day in the work carried on among the depressed classes the mass-movement is a prominent feature. The real success and its permanence depends on the extent to which the Missions are able to cope with the mulitudes that are pressing in by furnishing the instruction and guidance into Christian truth and Christian life that are necessary for the building up of a truly Christian community. The work of evangelization in such cases only begins when the multitudes have been gathered in. One is amazed when one reads of the numerous monastic centres which Columba succeeded in establishing throughout Scotland. These were his instruction centres by means of which those masses of the people were to be not only won but conserved for the faith.

Adamnan, who was ninth in succession to Columba in the abbacy of Iona and who began his rule exactly a hundred years after the death of the founder and was thus separated in age by about two generations from the completion of Columba's mission, must have been in a position to supply reliable information with regard to the facts of the mission of the saint. But when we turn to his *Life of St. Columba* to learn how this spiritual ambassador won the heart of this powerful savage monarch we find nothing but tales of miracles wrought by Columba in his approaches to the king. The entire plan of the " Life " is constructed ostensibly to exhibit his wonders in prophecy and in action. It is a glorification of the saint and not a history of the man. It is only when we come to the closing chapter of this work that we get into contact with the real human greatness of this man of God. The closing chapters of Adamnan's narrative are based on another *Life of Columba*, first appearing anonymously but ascribed to Cummein, the seventh Abbot, who began his rule sixty years after the death of Columba.

There are two pictures in the life of this great apostle of the faith that specially appeal to our imagination. One is that which depicts him as he first stood on the highest point of his new island home of Hi gazing, not regretfully backwards towards the land of his home from which he had exiled himself, but forward and outward to the heathen Scottish mainland and islands which he hoped to win to the obedience of the faith. The other is that of the closing day of his life when, no longer able to ascend to that modest height, he stood upon a little hill or mound situated above the site of the ancient monastery and with uplifted hands blessed it, adding with a truly prophetic vision of the future, "small and mean though this place is, yet shall it be held in great and unusual honour not only by the kings of the Scots and their people but also by the rulers of foreign and barbarous nations and their subjects."

Whatever amount of credence we may be willing to accord to Adamnan's and Cummein's narrative of other sayings and of angelic visitations and heavenly visions that marked that last day in the saint's life, the words which he is reported to have uttered regarding the honour in which his humble monastery would in future ages be held, we can have little hesitation in accepting as those of a prophet and seer who saw in the wondrous triumphs of the Gospel which he had proclaimed in heathen Scotland the promise of a world-wide victory of the faith. From whatsoever land he come, what Christian can read of that little isle made sacred by its memories of St. Columba or can tread its holy ground without experiencing some thrill of that emotion which found noble utterance in the words of Samuel Johnson which we have prefixed to this chapter of missionary history ?

For all Christians of this country this will always remain the most fascinating page in the history of Scotland. The missionary labours of Columba in Scotland extended over a period of thirty-four years. For the first two of those years his labours were confined to the region lying within easy reach of his chosen isle ; but in the year 565 Columba, accompanied by two other missionaries, both Irish Picts who were held in reputation as among the greatest saints of the time, crossed the mountain barrier of Drumalban and made his way to the court of Brude the Pictish king whose seat was near the river Ness. The king became a convert to the Christian faith and Columba remained in his kingdom for a time, establishing his monasteries among the Pictish tribes which, following the lead of the monarch, appear to have rapidly embraced the new faith.

The tales of the miraculous signs by which he overcame the hostility of the king and his priestly counsellors, which abound in the narrative contained in the writings of his biographers, are but the interpretation by an uncritical wonder-loving age of the singular power which flowed from his commanding personality and his consecrated life. Under the monk's robe there dwelt the heart of a king. " In him," writes Montalembert, " were the makings of a sailor, a soldier, poet and orator. To us looking back he appears a personage as singular as he is lovable, in whom through all the mists of the past and the cross-lights of legend, the man may still be recognized under the saint, a man capable and worthy of the supreme honour of holiness since he knew how to subdue his inclinations, his weakness, his instincts and his passions, and to transform them into docile and invincible weapons for the salvation of souls and the glory of God."

We can understand how such a personality subdued the resistance of kings and won unquestioning obedience from those who placed themselves under his leadership and authority ; but Columba would never have been Scotland's dearest saint unless behind all this there dwelt a power more potent than that which comes from intellectual or physical endowment, the power of self-sacrificing love clothed with humility. All this was embalmed in the name which he bore, Colum-cille, " the dove of the Church."

This chapter may fitly close with an extract from Adamnan's work in which by his touching narrative of the passing of the saint, which in its main features bears the stamp of truth, the author has atoned for the extravagances of the other parts of his story. After describing the aged saint's last tour of his settlement on the last day of his life, his visit to the barn, his rest half way on his journey back to the monastery, his encounter with the white pack-horse of the monastery which laid its head on his bosom, his ascent to the hill overlooking the monastery from which he blessed it in the words already quoted, he continues : " After these words he descended the hill and having returned to the monastery sat in his hut transcribing the Psalter and coming to that verse of the 33rd Psalm (in the English version Psalm 34), where it is written : ' They that seek the Lord shall want no manner of thing that is good,' ' Here,' said he, ' at the end of the page I must stop ; and what follows let Baithene write.' The last verse he had written was very applicable to the saint who was about to depart, and to whom eternal goods shall never be wanting. . . . Having written the aforementioned verse at the end of the page, the saint went to the church to the nocturnal vigils of the Lord's day and so soon as these were over, he returned to his chamber, and spent the remainder of the night on his bed where he had a bare flag for his couch and for his pillow a stone, which stands to this day as a kind of monument beside his grave. . . . As soon as the bell tolled at midnight, he rose hastily, and running more quickly than the rest he entered the Church alone

D

and knelt down in prayer beside the altar. Diarmit, his attendant, entering the church cried out in a mournful voice, ' Where art thou, father ? ' and feeling his way in the darkness, for the brethren had not yet brought in the lights, he found the saint lying before the altar ; and raising him up a little, he sat down beside him and laid his holy head on his bosom. And the saint, as we have been told by some who were present, even before his soul departed, opened wide his eyes and looked round him from side to side, with a countenance full of wonderful joy and gladness, no doubt seeing the holy angels coming to meet him. Diarmit then raised the holy right hand of the saint that he might bless his assembled monks. And the venerable father himself moved his hand at the same time as well as he was able that, as he could not in words, while his soul was departing, he might at least by the motion of his hand, be seen to bless his brethren. And having given them his holy benediction in this way, he immediately breathed his last."

WE now pass from what may well be called the Golden Age of Scottish Missionary History to a period of decay, a long period of gradual decay ending in an almost complete extinction of the missionary ideal which lent so much of its glory to the early Scottish Church. The influences which led to this period of eclipse came partly from within and partly from without the Church of Scotland. To the former belong those which are often associated with rapid and wide-spread success in great movements. Within the lifetime of the great leader in the evangelization of Scotland practically the whole country had become nominally Christian. Thus the inspiration to missionary effort which came from a surrounding heathenism was no longer present as on the day when Columba landed in Scotland on his great adventure. He had left a network of monastic establishments throughout the land which were intended to build up and consolidate the results of the mass-movement by which Scotland had been transformed from a pagan into a Christian country. For some generations these continued to operate along the lines which he laid down ; but they appear to have gradually lost the glow of their first enthusiasm, and the rapid decline of living religion throughout the nation in later days was no less striking than the rapid spread of Christianity in the earlier age. Not only was the horizon of the Church's vision confined within the bounds of the homeland, but even within this limited field the aggressive spirit of the first founders of the Church began to disappear. The nation remained Christian in name ; but " the salt had lost its savour."

The most serious influence, however, tending to produce this change came from without ; for, soon after the death of Columba, Rome began a determined and ultimately successful effort to deprive the Keltic Church of its independence and to bring it into submission to the Roman See. Attention has been already called to the fact that this Keltic

Church had developed its life and activities apart from the control of the Roman Church on lines of its own proceeding from the traditions of the early Church as those existed at a time when the Roman Church had not yet departed far from the apostolic ideal. The religion of the Keltic people was a simple Bible-Christianity. The Holy Scriptures were for them the rule of faith and life, and the study of the Scriptures was regarded as the first task of the teachers and ministers. In the fulfilment of this task they made use of the more important commentaries of the fathers and the older Latin translation, going back, however, also to the original Greek text. Over against the decrees of the Councils, which they did not go the length of absolutely rejecting, they asserted the higher authority of the Scriptures. Their Scripture-study took an essentially practical direction, their main endeavour being to bring their life into harmony with the precepts of Holy Writ. The Venerable Bede, one of the strongest opponents of the Keltic Church in the struggle begun with Rome's claim to supremacy, could hold up to his contemporaries no higher example of strict Christian morality, humility, self-denial, unworldliness and indefatigable zeal in the work of conversion than that of the Scottish monks. (*Hist. Eccl.* iii, 3–5.)

It was scarcely to be expected that the Romish Church, which was already on the path which was leading to the vision of the Church as a great world-power, would long suffer the Keltic Churches to remain independent of its sway. Its claim to be recognized as " Catholic " seemed to demand that those Churches should acknowledge the supremacy of the Bishop of Rome and persistent effort was begun to secure their submission.

There were three Church organizations to be dealt with, the ancient British Church which had its home in Wales, the Iro-Scottish Church in Ireland and the Alban-Scottish Church, the offshoot from the second which occupied the modern Scotland. Not only was it essential that those Churches should submit themselves to the Roman authority, but also that they should be compelled to abandon those usages which separated them in practice from the mother-church. The British Church was the first to succumb completely to this assimilating process. The coming of Augustin to England for the purpose of bringing about this assimilation was not immediately successful. A Conference with the British Church was held in the year 603. The representatives of the British Church were repelled by the arrogance of Augustin ; but, apart from this, the deadly hatred between Britons and Anglo-Saxons would have then rendered Church-fellowship between them impossible. The British Church continued to resist these Roman influences till in the year 768 one of their bishops gave way on the question of the date of Easter. A century later, when Wales came under the supremacy of King Alfred, the Abbot or Bishop of St. David's, with the consent of his clergy, placed his Church under Alfred's protection in order to its preservation from the plundering raids of the neighbouring princes. This opened the way for Anglo-Saxon influence, and a bishop of Llandaff consented to receive his consecration from the Archbishop of Canterbury. Still the process of absorption was very gradual. By the 12th century Wales had become almost completely " catholic." At the close of that century only a few pious monks of the old school bearing the name of

" Culdees " [1] were to be found. They had their monastery in the little island of Bardsey off the coast of Carnarvonshire.

The Romanizing process in the case of the Iro-Scottish Church was similar to that which has just been narrated ; but it was less rapid inasmuch as the deviation from Rome was there more pronounced than in Wales. The Irish Church had bishops but the country was not divided up into dioceses. The position of bishops in the monasteries living under the rule of an Abbot who often was a simple presbyter, was an anomaly which the Roman Church could not fit into its system, and besides this there were all the other divergences in regard to the date of Easter, the mode of tonsure, the question of the celibacy of the clergy, the mode of episcopal consecration, the form of the baptismal ceremony and many other details of ritual in worship. In the year 613 the successors of Augustin addressed a letter to the bishops and abbots of *Scotia* (i.e. of Ireland) which

---

[1] This was the name in common use in mediæval times to distinguish the followers of the old system from those of the Romanized Church. It is explained as the English equivalent of the old Keltic *ceile-de*, *keledei*, Latinized into *colidei* and has been interpreted to mean " servants of God."

raised the question of Easter. In consequence of this a deputation was sent by the Church in South Ireland to Rome which became convinced of the correctness of the Roman method of fixing the date of Easter and in 634 the Roman practice was adopted in South Ireland. Towards the end of this century through the influence of Adamnan, Abbot of Iona of that time, North Ireland was led also to accept the Roman method. In all other matters the Irish Church clung to its traditional practice. Years of controversy followed until the Church suffered a great eclipse through the Danish invasions.

The efforts of Rome were renewed in the middle of the 11th century. Normans who had settled in the south-east of Ireland placed themselves under the Archbishop of Canterbury. In 1074 Lanfranc consecrated the Bishop of Dublin and addressed a letter to the leading sovereign in which he complained of laxity in regard to the dissolution of marriage, the inadequate consecration of bishops *by a single bishop*, and baptism administered without the chrism. A decisive step was next taken by Pope Gregory VII, who addressed a rescript to the Irish (A.D.

1085) in which he asserted his supremacy as
the successor of St. Peter, and also sent a
papal legate to Ireland. But all these efforts
proved fruitless until the Archbishop of
Armagh, a friend of St. Bernard of Clairvaux,
allowed himself to be made the tool for the
carrying out of the Roman plans. In consequence of this he lost his see, but returning
as papal legate he succeeded in moving the
Irish to ask for the *pallium*, and in 1152
Ireland was divided into four archiepiscopal
and twenty-eight episcopal dioceses. In order
finally to establish the papal rule Pope
Adrian IV granted to Henry II permission
to conquer Ireland. When in 1172 the Irish
chiefs did homage at Cashel, the ecclesiastical
affairs of Ireland were adjusted to the demands
of Rome. Still here and there the Culdees
(*colidei*) lingered on for a time as in Wales.

The Keltic Church in Scotland was the last
to suffer this fate. Adamnan attempted, but
without the success he obtained in Ireland, to
move the monastery of Iona to adopt the
Roman Easter reckoning and to abandon the
old Keltic tonsure ; but in 710 the Pictish
king ordained that those changes should be
introduced throughout his dominions, and in

729, through the influence of Egbert, who spent thirteen years in Iona, Columba's monastery followed suit. Still in all essential respects there was no change in the constitution of the Church till Malcolm in 1057 ascended the Scottish throne. Queen Margaret, his consort, grand-daughter of Edmund Ironside, was devoted to the catholic faith and brought the Prior of Durham, Turgot, who was afterwards (1107) Bishop of St. Andrew's, to be her confessor. Alexander I, whose consort was a daughter of Henry I, continued the effort to assimilate the Scottish Church to the pattern of the Roman Church as it existed in England. He summoned a National Council at which Turgot was chosen as a bishop. He was consecrated by York ; but when he died (1115) Alexander applied to Canterbury for a successor who was consecrated by the Archbishop of Canterbury to the Scottish see of St. Andrews. This was a severe blow to the independence of the Keltic Church. Roman ritual and Roman monastic orders followed. Alexander took the Church of the Holy Trinity at Scone out of the hands of the Culdees, as the adherents of the old order were now designated, consecrated it to the Virgin and gave it to the Augustinians. David I (1124–53) was even more thorough-going in the changes which he effected. He founded the Bishopric of Glasgow, assigned to it churches and lands and appointed his tutor Johannes, who was prepared to intro-duce the Roman usages, to be its bishop. In addition he established seven other bishoprics and founded many abbeys and monasteries which he filled mainly with Cistercians. He endeavoured to Romanize the existing monasteries and churches with only partial success and had to leave the completion of this undertaking to his successors. In some places the Culdees were allowed to remain alongside Romish monks in the hope that they might be Romanized through the latter. Ultimately they were denounced as heretics and at the beginning of the 14th century the old order had practically vanished.

The record which has been given of this long struggle reveals the tenacity with which the ancient Keltic Church clung to its ancient tradition in Scotland and the deep impression which the ministrations of Columba had made upon the people. On the other hand it furnishes us with the explanation of the remarkable change which took place in the spirit of the Scottish Church when it emerged from the struggle defeated and robbed of its higher ideals in regard to the function of the Christian Church. For in proportion as the Scottish Church came under the influence of the Roman see its missionary spirit evaporated. The Roman Church had fallen away from the ideals which found expression in the missionary activity of the early centuries of its existence. It had come now to be regarded and reverenced as an end in itself rather than as the divinely appointed instrument for an end which was higher than itself, the establishment of the kingdom of God through the evangelization of the world. The missionary impulse had largely died out of the Church. The Church, now become a great world-power living for itself, had entered upon its dark age. In Scotland, this attitude once established, there followed a secularization of the Church more complete than that which had been reached in any other Church in Western Christendom. Religion in Scotland had been so closely bound up with the national life that the opportunities for this secularizing process were multiplied.

The Church of Scotland had become one of the wealthiest in Christendom. Half the wealth of the nation belonged to the clergy. Most of this was in the hands of the few individuals who, occupying the higher offices in the Church, had control of the whole body. Avarice, worldly ambition and the pomp of worldly greatness were manifest in all the high places of the Church. The ecclesiastical heads became the most powerful leaders in the government and policy of the nation. They wielded a secular power that meant much more to them than the spiritual authority which they possessed within the Church. Need we wonder that the missionary ideal disappeared and that nothing short of a complete revolution within the Church was needed to recover it ?

While the submission of the Scottish Church to the papal supremacy was the principal cause of this deterioration in the religious life of the Scottish nation, we must remind ourselves that, as has already been stated, there were also influences within the Church tending to render this possible. Long before this climax was reached the tide of religious life in Scotland become nominally Christian had begun to ebb. The Church which had been originally a mobilized army with its numerous strategic points had become organized on a peace footing. It continued to revere the heroic saints who had been its leaders in the great past ; but it was no longer facing their heroic tasks. Not that no work was needed to be done within the borders of its own Christianized land. The mass movements by which Christianity had been diffused throughout Scotland left ample room for a more intensive Christian work ; but while, no doubt, isolated examples of devotion to this form of Christian service were not lacking, the attitude of the Church as a whole was no longer that of an aggressive spiritual force but rather that of an institution bent on the continued maintenance of its own position. It lost its enthusiasm for those tasks which would have nourished and inspired life and prevented it from being drawn into the arena of secular ambition to become alternately the tool and the master of kings.

The era of Reformation arrived following in the wake of a great movement which touched many nations. It was in Scotland essentially a spiritual re-awakening of all classes among its people. The evangel was again heard in the land. The spirit of the best days of Scotland's past seemed to have returned. At such a time one might have expected as the fruit of such a reviving life, a recrudescence of the spirit of the ancient Scottish missionary Church ; but for more than two centuries there was little sign of its re-appearance. It is significant, however, that the Scottish Confession of 1560 bore on its front as motto and legend that word of our Lord which will always contain the charter of the Church's missionary enter-prise : " This gospel of the kingdom shall be preached in all the world for a witness unto all nations ; and then shall the end come." (*Matthew* xxiv, 14.) But generations were to pass before the Church which had placed its missionary obligation in the forefront of its Christian programme took any measures towards its fulfilment. Could it have been that, in that high moment of deliverance, the Scottish Church in proclaiming its recovered faith had caught some glimpse of the old vision? However this may have been, we know that the Church's vision must have quickly faded in the midst of that life-and-death struggle into which it was plunged in its long conflict with its nearer foes—the Church of Rome from whose fetters it had been emancipated and monarchs who sought to re-impose the yoke from which it had been freed.

It is noteworthy [1] also that, while in its Book of Common Order, the prayers contain many petitions for divine protection from the power of the Church of Rome and for the overthrow of that power, there is only one petition for the conversion of the heathen.

Confronted with the widespread ignorance regarding the very elements of Christian truth that prevailed among the people of Scotland in the days of the Reformation, the Church in the first period of its reawakened life had to address itself once more to the evangelization of Scotland and found its entire energies absorbed by this great task. We can scarcely wonder that under the pressure of such an absorbing duty the claims of the distant heathen were for the time forgotten by the Church. A century

---

[1] For this and some other particulars here noted see an excellent summary in *The Missions of the Church of Scotland*, by the Rev. Robert W. Weir (1900).

E

had to elapse before the Church reached a peaceful settled condition.

But even in the public documents of the Church belonging to this later period the references to the Church's missionary duty are both scanty and casual. The documents referred to are the Westminster Confession of Faith, and the Larger and Shorter Catechisms associated with it. In the Larger Catechism there is only one reference to the subject. It expounds the petition in the Lord's Prayer— " Thy kingdom come "—as including a prayer " that the Gospel may be propagated throughout the whole world, the Jews called and the fulness of the Gentiles be brought in." In the Directory for Public Worship published at the same time as the Confession of Faith and the two Catechisms, the minister is instructed to pray for " the propagation of the Gospel and the kingdom of Christ to all nations, the fall of Anti-christ and the hastening of the second coming of the Lord."

This expressed the *theoretical* attitude of the Church and it remained a merely theoretical attitude for another century and a half. When at the later date the first proposition for the active co-operation of the Church in missionary effort came before the Church, no one, as we shall see, of the strongest opponents of the proposal expressed any doubt as to the ultimate fulfilment of the divine purpose in the conversion of the world or as to the duty of ministers and their congregations to pray for it. But surely the missionary zeal of any Church is at a low ebb when it exhausts itself in the expression of a pious hope and the utterance of a formal prayer. As a matter of fact, the heathen world was at that time to the people of Scotland little more than a " geographical expression." Their contact with that world was of the slightest. It was not until some contact was established with an outlying world of real men and women sitting in darkness that the Church began to hear in the faintest measure the call of the heathen nations. To that period of renaissance and the movements which heralded its approach we now pass.

THE renaissance of the Missionary Ideal within the Scottish Church did not come with suddenness. It was preceded by some premonitory symptoms of an approaching change in the Church's conception of its responsibilities. When Scotland entered on its ill-fated Darien Expedition, with the fleets which it sent out it dispatched a number of ministers who were commissioned not only to preach to their countrymen, but also to evangelize the heathen of the land to which they were sent. The General Assembly of 1700 appears to have been more sympathetic in its attitude towards Foreign Missions than the General Assembly of nearly a century later, for in the letter which it addressed to the ministers who were being sent out with the expedition it expressed the hope that " the Lord will yet honour you and the

Church from which you are sent to carry the Name among the heathen."

This, however, can scarcely be regarded as a serious attempt to inaugurate a foreign missionary effort on the part of the Church. The work among the heathen occupied a very secondary place in the scheme. No serious effort had been made to prepare and equip a real Mission ; and the missionary side of the enterprise proved as great a failure as the commercial. No attempt was made to master the language of the people of the country to which the expedition was sent, and the scandalous behaviour of many members of the expedition did even more to frustrate the efforts of the ministers than any lack of equipment for the task assigned to them.

A few years later the Scottish Church was again brought into contact with the missionary enterprise. Following the example set by the institution, under the patronage of King William III, of the English Society for the propagation of Christian knowledge a movement was started in Scotland in 1707 for the foundation of a similar society. This society, like its English predecessor, while founded mainly for the purpose of providing Christian instruction for certain sections of the people in the home-land, included within its scope also missions to the heathen. The memorial which led to its foundation invited attention to the missionary labours of Elliot among the Indian tribes of North America, and also to the work of the Dutch missionaries. Not till 1717, however, did the society find itself possessed of any resources that could be applied to the purposes of a foreign mission.

Dr. Williams' bequest of an estate in Huntingdonshire to be transferred to the Scottish society, "three years after it should have sent three qualified ministers to infidel and foreign countries," encouraged the society to make preparation for a beginning of missionary effort. After much corres-pondence with the authorities in New England it engaged three missionaries to undertake work among the Indians. The Society ful-filled the conditions necessary for obtaining possession of the property bequeathed to it ; but in all other respects its first effort was unfortunate, for ultimately the three missionaries had to be recalled. Later the Society was fortunate in enlisting in its service the saintly David Brainerd (1743) who in the four succeeding years laboured with marked success. But the most fruitful result of the labours of this apostolic man was not the number of converts he had won, but the missionary enthusiasm which was awakened by his example and through the publication of his Diary. To this widely read Diary the Christian Church is indebted for many missionaries, in number exceeding the converts he had made.

In 1762 this Society asked the General Assembly of the Church of Scotland to appoint a collection on behalf of its Mission. This request was acceded to and the *first* collection for foreign missions within the Church of Scotland was made in that year. It amounted to a little over £500. Two years later the parish ministers were invited to raise funds for the establishment of schools for the education of the converted Indians and for the support of a native ministry. This effort resulted in the subscription of a sum of over £2,500, which in those days represented a large amount of liberality on the part of the donors and a great amount of effort on the part of the promoters of the scheme. It is interesting to note that among those who pleaded the claims of the scheme was an ordained Indian minister who was sent to Scotland from the North American Mission field.

The contributions of the Society to the work in America ceased with the outbreak of the American war ; but in 1783 they were resumed after the cessation of hostilities. It was found, however, that for a considerable number of years the Society had been contributing little or nothing to its foreign mission apart from interest on invested funds. Already in 1755 an apology for this apathy was presented in a sermon preached in St. Giles Church by Principal Robertson, who explained it as due to the demands made on the funds of the Society by its work in the Highlands and Islands. The reference which this preacher made to Missions on that occasion illustrates the prevailing attitude of the Church of the time. He discourses eloquently on the advances made in science among Christian nations as preparing the world for the reception of the Gospel. He speaks of the active and zealous spirits who had arisen and the societies they had organized for the propagation of the Gospel, and expresses the hope that " if it should please God to increase the number and to strengthen the hands of such well-disposed persons we might see the knowledge of the Lord filling the earth as the waters cover the sea." In all these general and grandiose pictures of the future no word of the present duty and responsibility of the Church of Scotland entrusted, as a part of the Christian Church, with a mission to the world ! Apologies for inaction have taken the place of action ; the Church is willing to leave its highest task to " zealous and active spirits " forming themselves into independent associations.

But while the Church still held aloof from official participation in missionary work, zealous and active spirits within it were not inactive. The closing years of the 18th century saw the birth of most of the chief missionary societies of Great Britain founded by zealous and active spirits in the various Churches of the land. In Scotland the ministers and members of the Church who had been touched by the rising tide of evangelical religion that was spreading itself widely over the country found an outlet for

the new life in similar societies formed by
them for the diffusion of the Gospel in heathen
lands.   The Scottish Missionary Society and
the Glasgow Missionary Society, both founded
in 1796, formed part of this wider movement.

In the same year this re-awakened interest
in the spread of Christianity among non-
Christian nations made itself heard within
the courts of the Church of Scotland.   Two
Synods, the Synod of Fife and the Synod of
Moray sent up overtures to the General
Assembly on the subject of Foreign Missions.
The overture from the Synod of Fife was of
a general character ; it asked the Assembly
" to consider of the most effective method by
which the Church of Scotland may contribute
to the diffusion of the Gospel over the world."
The other was expressed in more specific
terms ; it asked for an " Act of Assembly for
a general collection throughout the Church
to aid the several societies for propagating
the Gospel among the heathen nations."
The discussion in the House turned mainly
on the latter.

As the aims and constitution of the
missionary societies figure so largely in this
historical debate, especially in the speeches

of those who opposed the missionary overtures, it will be of advantage at this point to refer to the origin of the societies alluded to in the course of the discussion. The discussion itself will be considered at greater length on account of the light which it throws on the currents of religious and political thought which at that time were stirring the mind of Scotland.

The latter years of the 18th century were marked by notable events in the political and intellectual life of Europe ; in Great Britain they were accompanied by a remarkable quickening of religious life within the evangelical Churches.

Early in the century the United Brethren of Moravia had led the way in missionary enterprise and had found the key to a high spiritual life in missionary endeavour. In Great Britain, as we have seen, there were founded societies which recognized, but with only a faint and halting recognition, the claims of such endeavour to a place in the Christian programme. Any efforts which these societies made were only slight and short-lived. It was only when the century was drawing to a close that the modern

missionary age began in this country. The
missionary societies which then came into
being are, most of them, in full and fruitful
operation in all the world to-day, while
others have been absorbed into the Church
system in the lands in which they had their
birth.

In 1786 the Wesleyans began their work
among the negroes of the West Indies. In
1792 the Baptist Missionary Society, under
the inspiring initiative of William Carey and
the ministers who met at Kettering, started
on its great career. In the year following,
Carey sailed for India where he laid the
foundation of its Indian Mission and opened
up a path of entrance into India for all who
were to follow. In 1795 the London
Missionary Society was constituted, the result
of an appeal which came from a meeting of
ministers of various denominations inviting
brethren throughout the land to consider the
practicability of forming a missionary institution " that should sink all party names and
inferior distinctions in the one great design
of sending the Gospel to heathen and other
unenlightened nations."

At the second general meeting of this

society it passed a resolution as to the fundamental principles of its future operations
which includes the following remarkable
pronouncement : " It shall be left (as it ought
to be left) to the minds of the persons whom
God may call into the fellowship of His Son
from among them to assume for themselves
such form of Church government as to them
shall appear most agreeable to the word of
God." The principle here laid down, which
one hears to-day proclaimed in some quarters
as a new discovery of our modern age, is thus
seen to be as old as the very beginning of the
missions that are at work in the world to-day.
Many of the Churches which are working
side by side in India and China and in other
mission fields have come to recognize the
necessity as well as the wisdom of the principle
enunciated so long ago, and the efforts which
are now being made to bring about union
amongst the Churches which have grown up
in those fields are the logical result of the
acceptance of this principle. And from the
Mission field in turn has come one of the
strongest influences making for re-union
among the Churches at home.

Scotland was speedily touched by the same

influences which re-awakened England to a
sense of its missionary responsibility and in
the spring of 1796 the two sister societies
already referred to, one in Edinburgh and one
in Glasgow, were founded.   Dr. Erskine, who
figures prominently in the debate in the
Assembly which is now to be described,
preached the first annual sermon on behalf
of the newly formed Scottish Missionary
Society to a crowded congregation in St.
Andrew's Church, Edinburgh, the Church
which half a century later was to be
the scene of the Disruption which led
to the formation of the Free Church of
Scotland.

Of the debate in the General Assembly of
1796 we have two independent accounts ;
one published anonymously in the year of
the Assembly, the authorship of which was
ascribed to Mr. Robert Heron,[1] the ruling
elder from Galloway who figures prominently
in the debate, the other dating from 1841

---

[1] Mr. Heron's pamphlet, which extends to 74 pages, sets out to
give a full report of the debate.   It was composed immediately
after the debate had taken place and is of special value as a
contemporary document written by one who saw and heard
all that was said and done on that memorable day.   This
pamphlet is very rare, only three copies having been known to
exist in recent times.

from the pen of Hugh Miller, on which Dr. Robert Buchanan based the narrative given in his *Ten Years' Conflict*.

The fate of the overtures will appear in the narrative that follows. In the first place it was agreed to consider them jointly. After two members had spoken in support of the overtures but without submitting a motion, Mr. Heron, the reputed author of the report of the discussion which was subsequently published, addressed the Assembly. After a long dissertation on the beneficial influence of Christianity on society and the individual, including a rather irrelevant excursion into the question of the causes of the downfall of the Roman Empire (let us remember that this was the age of Gibbon) in the course of which he was called to order by the Moderator, he confined himself to remarks on the appropriateness of the action recommended to the Church by these overtures in view of the new spirit favourable to the diffusion of the Gospel that had been manifested in so many quarters, and the circumstances that had arisen favourable to the carrying out of the new desire that had been awakened amongst Christian people. Maintaining that there was a strong case for entertaining the overtures, he concluded by moving "that a Committee be appointed to inquire into and deliberate upon the overtures and to report the result of such inquiry and deliberation to next General Assembly."

Dr. Erskine in a single sentence seconded the motion. The Rev. Mr. Hamilton of Gladsmuir, who had come, evidently eager to oppose the overtures, (for he rose to speak at the same moment with Dr. Erskine, the seconder of the motion) followed Dr. Erskine, and in a long speech, evidently prepared and delivered with a view to oratorical effect, addressed the Assembly. Some passages from this speech may be quoted as they are most illuminating with regard to the views that were then prevalent in some quarters on the subject of Missions, as they are prevalent in similar quarters to-day. "To spread abroad," he declared "the knowledge of the Gospel among barbarous and heathen nations seems to me highly preposterous, in as far as it anticipates, nay, as it even reverses the order of nature. Men must be polished and refined in their manners before they can be properly enlightened in religious truths.

Philosophy and learning must in the nature of things take the precedence. Indeed it would hardly seem less absurd to make revelation precede civilization in the order of time than to pretend to unfold to a child the *Principia* of Newton ere he is made at all acquainted with the letters of the alphabet." Quoting the verse " A man is to be judged according to what he hath, not according to what he hath not," he said that " this gracious declaration of Scripture ought to liberate from groundless anxiety the minds of those who stated in such moving language the condition of the heathen." After descanting on the simple virtues of the untutored Indian or Otaheitan, he continued : " But go engraft on his simple manners the customs, refinements, and may I add, the vices of civilized society, and the influence of that religion which you give as a compensation for the disadvantages attending such a communication will not refine his morals nor ensure his happiness." The dangers attending the proclamation of the doctrine of salvation not by good works but by faith were then depicted. " If," said the speaker, " the danger of misapplying this doctrine in the

F

interests of immorality is so common among
people instructed by stated and regular
pastors and early embued with a pious and
virtuous education, how can we entertain a
rational doubt that the wild inhabitants of
uncivilized regions would use it as a handle
for the most flagrant violation of justice and
morality ? " " The history of God's revelation was in conformity," he maintained,
" with the principle he advocated.   The Jews
had to be transformed by slow, very slow,
degrees from a rude people into an enlightened
nation dwelling in the very centre of the
civilized world before they could be intrusted
with the brighter dispensation of the Christian
faith.   The apostle Paul preached, not to
naked savages, but to the inhabitants of
cultured cities."   In closing his speech he
added : " In view of the spiritual destitution
and general ignorance prevailing in our own
country, with the stream of infidelity and
licentiousness that is spreading its influence
among the multitude, fed by that of a
neighbouring country (the reference is to
France and the Revolution) swelled into a
raging flood, threatening to make a dismal
wreck of everything glorious that our country

contains, all the talents and zeal of every sincere Christian were needed for our own land."

The scarcity which involved so much suffering among the poor was summoned to his aid by the speaker as an argument against the ordering of a collection in aid of missionary societies. He denounced the action of those ministers " who had set apart for this purpose funds collected for the poor," and declared " that such ministers laid themselves open not only to ecclesiastical censure but also to penal prosecution." After this remarkable declamation Mr. Hamilton moved that in place of the motion before the Assembly be substituted the motion " that the overtures from the Synods of Fife and Moray be immediately dismissed."

Dr. Erskine then rose to reply. Before proceeding to discuss the motions before the House he demanded that the last speaker should specify the guilty persons to whom he referred in his closing remarks and the circumstances of the cases alluded to. Mr. Hamilton in response to the cry " Explain, explain," endeavoured to soften the harshness of his accusation by saying that as the church-door collections were set apart for the poor it was unwarrantable to apply them to any other purpose. He explained that he did not mean that money " expressly and professedly " collected for the poor had been otherwise applied.

Dr. Erskine resuming said that he had " no difficulty in vindicating himself and his brethren from the odious insinuation made by the preceding speaker. The collections referred to had been made on extraordinary occasions and specifically for Missions." He enunciated at the same time a principle to which at a later date Chalmers gave magnificent expression and one which needs to be impressed upon the mind of the Church to-day, namely, that voluntary contributions for such purposes instead of taking from the scanty pittance of the indigent adds to it by keeping the mind alive to the feelings of sympathy and charity. After some rather unsympathetic remarks regarding the missions of the Roman Catholic Church which might fitly have been omitted, he recounted the achievements of the missions established by the societies which have been above mentioned. Replying to the contention of the previous speaker, he said that he had always considered it the peculiar glory of Christianity that it was adapted alike to the learned and the unlearned. After quoting a number of Scripture passages in illustration of this he reminded the Assembly of St. Paul's utterance in the words[1] : " I am debtor both to the Greeks and to the Barbarians." He swept aside the specious argument based on the alleged scarcity by pointing

---

[1] In Hugh Miller's narrative a dramatic touch is given to it at this point. He records that Dr. Erskine, turning towards the Moderator, exclaimed, " Rax me that Bible," and read from it the apostle's declaration.   Dr. Robert Buchanan in his *Ten Years' Conflict* follows Hugh Miller's narrative and includes in his account the dramatic episode.   Hugh Miller's narrative appeared in 1841, Mr. Heron's in 1796 immediately after the meeting of Assembly.   The latter gives the simple quotation from the apostle's letter to the Romans.   Hugh Miller's form of the story has always made a strong appeal to the Scottish imagination and many would be grieved if it had to be abandoned.   But historical criticism has laid its cold hand on some of the sayings that have been long cherished. The familiar story of Galileo, as he rises from his knees after reciting his humiliating and abject recantation of his doctrine regarding the motion of the earth, muttering, " *Eppur si muove* " (it moves, nevertheless), has been abandoned, although told with delight by his earlier biographers.   It is difficult to understand how one who was so entirely in sympathy with the old divine could have omitted a graphic touch which would have lent so much impressiveness to his story, as it is also difficult to believe that a writer of Hugh Miller's candour and truthfulness could have invented it to embellish his narrative. These two improbabilities seem to balance each other and we may justly conclude that Hugh Miller found the story current when he wrote and accepted it on the ground of its inherent probability.   Perhaps we cannot do better than follow his example, although with some hesitation.

to the extravagance and luxury that was so conspicuous in the society of the day, adding that a wish to benefit our fellow creatures in distant regions and a donation for that purpose, instead of lessening, would increase the compassion of the generous to the needy at home.

Dr. Carlyle, the minister of Inveresk, known in the annals of the period as " Jupiter Carlyle," then rose to endorse the views propounded by Mr. Hamilton, whose motion for the immediate dismissal of the overtures he cordially seconded. He remarked that for half a century he had been a member of the Assembly and yet this was the first time he remembered to have heard such a proposal made as that contained in the overtures and that he could not help thinking it was the worst time for making it. " As clergymen," he added, " let us pray that Christ's kingdom may come as, we are assured, it shall come in the course of providence."

Dr. Hill, Principal of St. Mary's College in the University of St. Andrew's, who was then the leader of what was known as the " Moderate " party in the Church of Scotland, followed soon after with a speech in general support of the motion for dismissal but suggesting an amended form of motion. He directed his opposition mainly to the overture from the Synod of Moray, denouncing in unmeasured and exaggerated terms both the spirit and the methods of the missionary societies referred to in the overture. He seemed to place them in the same category with certain political movements of the time which, he said, were attempts against our happy constitution, against the order of everything we possess and hold dear. He dreaded the results which would flow from a proposal that these missionary societies should correspond with all societies which had the same end in view and should co-operate with them to the extent even of combining their resources. With changes of membership which were inevitable, it was not unreasonable to dread that the common fund might be perverted from its original channel and be made the means of stirring up temporal strife instead of promoting spiritual peace. " All true Christians," he said, " are united in prayer for, and the confident belief in, the future arrival of the glorious era when the earth shall be filled with the knowledge of the Lord as the waters cover the sea ! " He exhorted ministers to instruct and set a pious example before their flocks, to train them up for immortality, that they might transmit to their children and their children's children the religion which they themselves had received as their dearest inheritance. " These children," he said, " scattered in various quarters of the world, will carry along with them, wherever they may go, the religion of the Lord Jesus Christ in their hearts and in their lives." This was Principal Hill's missionary programme. The subsequent history of numbers of his countrymen in heathen lands is a strange commentary on this unique scheme for the evangelization of the world.

Still Principal Hill was not satisfied, he confessed, with the curt dismissal of the overtures. He was of opinion that the Assembly, while dismissing the overtures, should express its regard for the object of these overtures and the reasons which had influenced the action of those who had submitted them. Dr. Hill accordingly moved the following deliverance : " The General Assembly considered the overtures and judging it highly inexpedient at this time to appoint a Collection over Scotland by the General Assembly and not considering the circumstances of the time as favourable for the General Assembly's adopting any particular measures, dismiss the same ; at the same time recommend to all members of the Church of Scotland in their different stations to use every competent means of promoting within the sphere of their influence the knowledge of the Gospel, a just sense of the inestimable benefits it conveys to all those who embrace it and the practice of those virtues by which Christians make their light shine before men. And while they offer fervent prayers to Almighty God for the fulfilment of His promise in giving the Son the heathen for His inheritance, they resolve that they will embrace with thankfulness any future opportunity of contributing by their exertions to the propagation of the Gospel of Christ which Divine Providence may hereafter open."

At this point Dr. Carlyle again intervened and urged the passing of the simple motion for the immediate dismissal of the overtures.

Thereupon David Boyle, Esq., Advocate, ruling elder for the burgh of Irvine (subsequently Lord President of the Court of Session), rose and delivered in a speech disfigured by intemperate language and unjustifiable insinuation an attack on the missionary societies as having laid the foundations of political societies which had disturbed the peace and tranquillity of the country.

The Rev. Dr. William Taylor of Glasgow discovered a new reason for supporting Dr. Hill's motion in the fact that the proposal for a missionary collection was not properly before the House inasmuch as no petition for national aid had been received. He then fell back on the well-worn argument that the Church had enough to occupy it at home, and he called upon it to employ its zeal in combating the spread of infidelity, for example in counteracting the influence of " that infidel and profane book recently published, *The Age of Reason*, by Thomas Paine, which had insinuated much of its poison among the very lowest ranks of society for whom indeed it seems alone calculated." This would be, he held, employing zeal in a more promising cause than the dubious and difficult one of sending away our men and money to a foreign land.

The Assembly now became impatient for a division, was indisposed to listen to further discussion, and after one or two members had made a dignified protest against the insinuations contained in the future Lord President's speech and against the dictatorial tone which he had used, the Assembly divided, with the result that the motion for dismissal (in the form submitted by Principal Hill) was carried by 58 votes against 46 in favour of the motion to appoint a Committee.

Perhaps it may seem that unnecessary prominence has been given in our narrative to this debate in the General Assembly, and that the discussion has been presented in too minute detail. But this course has been adopted for several important reasons. First of all, because it is one of the most vivid pictures which has been preserved to us of the Church of Scotland as it was at the close of the 18th century. There are no records of that time which exhibit so clearly the currents of thought and feeling that were running at that time in the life of the Scottish Church and indeed of the Scottish nation. Further, in studying the history of the missionary ideal in the Scottish Churches it is necessary to understand what it had to encounter in the way of opposition, open and avowed, as well as the subtle smiling obstruction of the indifferent who scorned all great enthusiasms. In the debate which has been described every shade of feeling which was characteristic of the various sections of the Church is revealed, from the arrogant and cast-iron Toryism of the Lord President, the scarcely veiled paganism of the oration of the young minister who spoke as if fresh from some college debating society, and the cold but believing moderatism of the Principal of St. Mary's, to the warm evangelism of the learned and venerable Dr. Erskine. One feels as one studies this record to-day how far the entire Scottish Church has moved since 1796. The next chapter will deal with this advance.

THE scene which has been described in the preceding chapter could not be reproduced to-day in any Church entitled to be called Christian for the missionary ideal has now embedded itself in that name. Yet, notwithstanding the advance which has taken place in the general conception of the functions of the Christian Church, we have to recognize the continued presence of the various types of thought which came to open expression in that notable Assembly which was for the moment successful in excluding Missions from the sphere of the organized action of the Scottish Church. Who has not heard and does not still hear to-day the oft-reiterated contention that so long as ignorance and irreligion prevail at home the expenditure of the men and money of the Church on Foreign

Missions is without justification ? And this contention will continue to make itself heard so long as the Church has to face within its own borders an imperfect loyalty to its Lord and distrust in the power of His Gospel ; for this apparent zeal for the interests of the Church at home is the fair garb with which these are wont to clothe themselves.

The still more fundamental contention heard in that Assembly, namely, that it is unnecessary, unwise and even dangerous to bring the disturbing forces of a new religion into the midst of heathen peoples living in the primitive simplicity of an untutored barbarism, is advanced to-day, as it was then, with all the embellishment which ignorance of the realities of uncivilized life makes possible. These are the commonplaces of anti-missionary propaganda uttered to-day with unmasked boldness in the camp of the enemy outside, inducing in the minds even of professing Christians a secret hesitancy and misgiving in regard to the foreign missionary enterprises of the Church. But these are rarely heard in the courts of the Church. With the more extended knowledge that has now been reached with reference to the

religious cults of the nations, especially of
those which have inherited an ancient civilization, this latter contention appears in a
new and more plausible guise in the modern
proposition that each nation has evolved for
itself the religion that is best suited to its
needs and should be left in undisturbed
possession of it ; in short that the claim of
Christianity to be a universal religion must
be abandoned. The germ of each one of
these contentions can be found in the speeches
from which quotations have been given in
the preceding chapter. There was in them, in
addition to all this, an element of fear, real
or assumed, arising out of the special circumstances of the time. The re-awakening of the
spirit of liberty in that age, of which the
most arresting example was seen in the
French Revolution, had resulted in the formation of political societies which filled with
alarm the upholders of the old order. To
some the growth and multiplication of such
associations seemed to be a prelude to the
repetition in their own country of the excesses
and horrors which followed in the wake of
the revolutionary movement in France. All
societies, philanthropic and missionary as

well as political, were placed by those
alarmists in the same category. In their
panic they had lost the power of discrimi-
nation. Missionary societies thus came under
the ban and shared the same condemnation.
Of this unreasoning panic the future Lord
Justice-General was the most conspicuous
example. One wonders how any judicial
mind could have shewn such inability to
discriminate between revolutionary associations and missionary societies ; but there
is no limit to the length of unreason to which
panic is able to carry its victims.

Yet, to those who can look beneath the
surface and can see beyond the outward
temporary result, this debate presents another
side. It ended in a defeat which was really
the beginning of a victory. The fact that the
missionary overtures were dismissed by only
a small majority is important, for it proved
the large extent to which the Scottish Church
had shared in the spiritual movements of the
time. When the state of religion existing at
that time in the Churches of Europe is
remembered one can scarcely hesitate to
accept the statement that " in probably no
other Church of the age could such a result

(i.e., so favourable to the cause of missions) have been seen."

Let it also be noted that very many of those who were responsible for the dismissal of the overtures shrank from a bare dismissal which would have had the effect of a disavowal of their interest in the diffusion of Christianity among the nations. They were unable to rid themselves of the feeling that the cause which they would thus have seemed to be arresting had behind it a divine sanction which they durst not ignore. Accordingly the deliverance of the Assembly, while it dismissed those particular overtures, did not dismiss the missionary cause by the terms in which it was expressed. It may have looked as if the Assembly in order to save the face of the Church had inserted an empty and merely formal recognition of the faith of the Church in the ultimate spread of the Gospel throughout the world ; but it is more charitable and probably also truer to believe that it was due as much to a conviction that the Church was by its name and purpose committed to the missionary cause and a premonition that it would soon have to face this wider responsibility. One would like to think that, when

G

those clauses were added to the original curt and bald motion for dismissal, we were given a glimpse of the soul of the Church working its way slowly and with extreme caution to ultimate fuller expression. The subsequent history of the Church of Scotland confirms this view. The deliverance spoke of a future opportunity and within a generation that opportunity came. Amongst the foremost in calling upon the Church to use its opportunity and launch out into a great missionary enterprise were some of those who had taken part in the dismissal of that opportunity which came so many years before.

In spite of the dismay with which one peruses the record of that lost opportunity, when one surveys the developments which came later and all that has issued from them in the great mission fields of the world, one cannot fail to recognize in this many-phased period of the history of the Church of Scotland the presence of God's guiding hand. God moves in a mysterious way in his dealings not only with individuals but also with His Church.

Without suggesting the slightest extenuation of the Church's failure to recognize the

the great opportunity which came to it in 1796, one cannot resist the impression that even the apathy of that time was overruled by the Church's Head to an end that lay beyond the horizon of both parties in the Assembly of that year.   One can well imagine that, if the particular proposals sent to that Assembly had been entertained, the course of missionary history in Scotland might have followed a different line from that which it ultimately took and with a result more restricted than that which has been actually achieved. If the church had started its missionary enterprise along the line suggested, namely, by aiding missionary societies existing outside its regular organization, it might have failed to attain to that higher conception of the Church as itself the missionary society and as exercising its highest function in the maintenance and direction of its own missionary activities.   This is the position which the Church ultimately reached and this goal was in sight when, in the better days which soon came, it began to gird itself for its new task and rested not till it gave to its Foreign Mission a place in the forefront of its operations.

Foreign writers on the history of Missions have noted this as a distinguishing feature of the Missions of the Scottish Churches and have added the statement that Scotland is the only country in which the national Church has incorporated the work of Missions in its organization. It would have been more correct to say that this is a distinctive feature which it possesses in common with other Presbyterian Churches for it is found also in other countries in Churches which follow the Presbyterian Order.

Many advantages in other respects have been claimed for the episcopal system ; but it does not lend itself to missionary organization in the same degree of completeness that has been attained under the Presbyterian constitution. The Church of England, for example, works through two great missionary societies, the Society for the Propagation of the Gospel (S.P.G.) and the Church Missionary Society (C.M.S.), both of which are exerting a wide influence in many mission fields ; but this method of carrying on its missionary operations does not express with the same objective distinctness the missionary ideal of the Church. Thus has God turned the defeat of that early effort to bring the Church of Scotland into contact with Missions into a victory by ultimately securing for them their restoration to their original place among the organized activities of the Christian Church.

Apart from the fact that this is ideally their rightful place, practically it has been the means of leading them to greater achievement. If it be true, as has sometimes been said, that in proportion to their membership and their resources the Scottish Churches have a larger place in the missionary world than most other Churches, with the exception of the Moravian Church, this is to be attributed not to superiority in spirituality and devotion to their Lord, but largely to the place which they have been led to give to Missions in the scheme of Church life and to the facilities which their ecclesiastical organization has provided for the realization of their ideal. Once its Foreign Mission had secured this place *within* the Church of Scotland there was ready to hand the organization that was needed for enlisting the aid of its members in the near and remote parts of the land. Its presbyteries could be called to the aid of

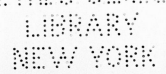

the Church in the work of interesting congregations in its missionary efforts and of securing
a steadily growing revenue for the maintenance
of a continuously expanding work in an
ever-widening field. Year by year the
Scottish Churches have found the advantage
of presbyterial organization in the diffusion
of an interest in Missions and have been
endeavouring to render it more efficient.
Centralization has its advantages and is
needed for administrative purposes ; but it
depends for its usefulness on the extent to
which it can devolve and diffuse a sense of
responsibility throughout the whole Church.
Presbyteries have in many cases done
invaluable service to the cause of Missions ;
but they may yet have to be charged with
still greater responsibility if the Church is
to cope with the demands of its growing
work.

In addition to all this the place which the
foreign Mission holds within the Church has
made it possible for it to secure for its Mission
fields a force of highly educated and well-
equipped workers. Its missionaries do not
constitute a distinct or inferior order of its
clergy ; they are ministers of the Church

sharing all the rights and privileges of their
brethren in the Church at home, and have
frequently been recruited from the ranks of
its most distinguished students and graduates.
This close organic connection between the
missionary and the Church is also a strength
and inspiration to those who are thus sent
forth. The missionary is the servant of the
Church of Christ, not the agent of a society
and exposed to the consequences of its
fluctuations in mood and policy. Moreover
he may, while at home, possess full or associate
membership in the Committee to which the
Church has entrusted the conduct of its
Mission affairs. This cordial and confidential
relation between the missionary and the home
base has been attended with the best results
and has raised the *esprit de corps* of the
missionary armies in the field.

From this digression, in which the position
reached by the vote of 1796 has been sur-
veyed and contrasted with that at which
the Church, a generation later, found itself,
it is necessary to return to the history that
lay between those two periods. When the
tide begins to flow the incoming wave
breaks upon the shore and seems to have

its fragments gathered back into the receding waters. But soon it is followed by another which advances a little way beyond the limit reached by its precursor, and thus in continuous succession each incoming wave repeats this advance—because far out behind these wavelets is the mighty force of the moving main.

To the rebuff which the missionary societies suffered at the hand of the Scottish Church they replied by launching, with a resoluteness that had grown more intense, the effort for which they had been preparing. Having searched eagerly for suitable fields in the non-Christian world, they selected the Muhammadan population of Karass, a province in Eastern Russia, and Sierra Leone in Africa, and subsequently a Mission to Western India came to be added.

The Czar of Russia, Alexander I, was well-affected to Protestant Missions and offered special facilities to the pioneers of Scottish Missions in the province of Karass. But both the African and the Russian Missions were short-lived by reason of outward difficulties in the one case and internal dissensions in the other. Only the Mission to India endured ;

it continues to this day in the Western India Mission of the United Free Church of Scotland.

In 1821 the Glasgow Missionary Society which had previously confined its efforts to helping other societies, especially the Scottish Missionary Society, by means of financial assistance, opened up a Mission of its own in Africa which was destined to permanence. It chose Kaffraria as its field and there it laid the foundation of those Missions with which the Free Church of Scotland and the United Presbyterian Church were, in the years before their union to form the United Free Church, long identified. These became the *nuclei* of the extensive Mission in S. Africa now carried on by the United Free Church.

We return to India in the opening up of which to missionary effort the Scottish Missionary Society played an important part. The closing years of the 18th century had witnessed in Scotland a noble effort of self-sacrifice in the cause of missions, when Robert Haldane of Airthry parted with the whole of his estate in order to found an Indian Mission in Benares, the sacred city of the Hindus. Inspired by accounts of the success of Carey's work in India Haldane

planned a thoroughly equipped Mission to
which he was prepared to devote his resources.
His heroic purpose was frustrated by the
refusal of the Directors of the East India
Company to permit the agents of the projected
Mission to enter India—a refusal from which
all the great influence which Haldane had at
his command failed to move them.   Haldane
had selected for the scene of his operations
the very centre of Hindu superstition and
fanaticism and the East India Company,
dreading the disturbance which they considered likely to be produced in their dominions by
such an attempt on the strongholds of Hinduism, remained obdurate in their opposition.

A few years later the Scottish Missionary
Society made its entrance into India with a
scheme less ambitious and more wisely
conceived.   It chose Western India as its
field.   Its objective was Bombay and along
with this Poona, the capital of the Peshvas,
which a few years before had been added,
together with the Maratha kingdom of which
it was the centre, to the territory under the
Company's rule ; but the Society's missionaries, had, in the first instance, to content
themselves with making a beginning in a

district less conspicuous, in which their operations were likely to cause less alarm to the
authorities. While refusing them permission
to begin work in the capital, the Government
of Bombay allowed them to open stations in
the district lying along the sea-coast to the
south of Bombay known as the South Konkan.
But while labouring in this inconspicuous
field they remained on the alert, kept their
eye constantly on Bombay and Poona, and
when the auspicious moment arrived for
obtaining an entrance into these cities,
transferred themselves with alacrity to these
important centres and founded the Missions
which to-day as Missions of the Scottish
Churches continue the work which the patience
and tact of those pioneer missionaries made it
possible to establish.

There is a touch of romance in the manner
in which, a little over a century ago, this first
Scottish Mission in India began. The missionaries sent out by the Scottish Society were all
ordained ministers of the Church of Scotland.
The first of these was the Rev. Donald
Mitchell, son of the minister of the remote
parish of Ardclach, a few miles distant from
Nairn and situated within the bounds of

the Synod which addressed its famous overture to the General Assembly of 1796. But Donald Mitchell's early career had nothing in it to suggest the pioneer of Scottish Missions to India. Near the close of his career as a student in preparation for the ministry of the Church of Scotland his faith became so overclouded by religious doubt that he felt constrained to turn aside to a secular career. Obtaining a cadetship in the East India Company he went out to India to serve as an officer in the army of the Honourable East India Company. While stationed in Gujarat he came in contact with a missionary of the London Missionary Society which at that time was carrying on the Mission which was subsequently handed over to the Presbyterian Church of Ireland. This missionary was instrumental in leading the young officer back to faith, and in the joy of his recovered faith he resolved to dedicate himself to the service of his Lord as a missionary to the people of India. Having resigned his commission he returned without delay to Scotland, completed his unfinished theological course, and in 1822 was ordained by the Presbytery of Nairn as a missionary of the Scottish Missionary Society to India. He reached Bombay in January; 1823, and soon after began his work in the Konkan at Bankot, known in the East India Company's records as Fort Victoria. After a few months of indefatigable labour in which he had the assistance of three colleagues, who followed him out to India in the same year, his health gave way and in November of the same year he succumbed to a long-continued attack of fever while being removed by his colleagues to a healthier region above the Western Ghâts. His last halting place was the village of Poladpur, picturesquely situated on the banks of the Savitri and under the shadow of the massive heights of Mahabaleshvar ("the god of great strength") on the summit of which now stands Bombay's chief sanatorium. There in that village Donald Mitchell's brief missionary career came to a close. His last words uttered just as he was passing breathed the hope which had guided his steps to India as a missionary of the Cross: "The earth shall be full of knowledge of the Lord. Amen and Amen." Most of this the traveller passing through this village may learn if he turns aside to visit the lonely grave and reads the inscription carved on the tombstone which marks the sacred spot. The Government of Bombay, which in the days of the East India Company excluded the missionary from its capital city, has now constituted itself the guardian of his tomb. This band of pioneer missionaries increased rapidly in number until in 1839 the Society had sent out seven missionaries, the last of these being Dr. John Wilson who landed in India in 1829. The years 1830 and 1831 saw both Bombay and Poona occupied. This was the reply of the missionary societies to the challenge that came to them from the apathy of the Church.

How fared it with the Church during this interval? When people generally had recovered from the panic which the rise of societies stirred by political aims had created, their fear of the missionary societies also disappeared. To this the increasing circulation of information regarding the work of these societies, the dissemination of periodicals containing tidings from the mission field and of the biographies of eminent missionaries such as Henry Martyn largely contributed. It is indeed no exaggeration to say that the evangelical life of Scotland was nourished largely by its missionary literature ; so intimate is the relation between the well-being and the well-doing of the Christian Church.

When in 1813 the time for renewing the charter of the East India Company arrived and the charter came under revision, among the hundreds of petitions which were presented praying that provision should be made in the new charter for the opening up of India to missionary enterprise, the first to be lodged was that of the Church of Scotland. The Church of Scotland petitioned also for the appointment of Presbyterian chaplains for India. Both petitions achieved their object.

It is interesting to note that the first chaplain to be thus appointed, Dr. Bryce, was the first to make a definite proposal to the Church of Scotland that it should undertake direct missionary work in India. In 1823 Dr. Bryce addressed an elaborate memorial on this subject from Calcutta to the General Assembly. When Dr. Bryce went to India he appears to have entertained little hope of the success of direct missionary work in that country ; but his interest in missionary work was awakened soon after his arrival in Calcutta through his contact with the educated classes of the Indian community. The result was his appeal which was presented to the General Assembly of 1824.

It was evident that the "future opportunity" referred to in the deliverance of 1796 had now arrived, for at the same time with this memorial came a large number of overtures from Synods (including the Synod of Moray, still loyal to the missionary cause), and from Presbyteries inviting the Church to establish a Foreign Mission. These all came up for discussion on the 27th May, the anniversary of the day on which the first overtures had been so summarily disposed of. It is, further, noteworthy that on this occasion the motion for the adoption of the overtures came from Dr. Inglis, the leader of the party which had, on the former occasion, been responsible for the rejection of the missionary proposals. In moving the deliverance he referred to the debate of 1796, reminding the Assembly that the resolution then adopted contained a pledge on the part of the Church to proceed to missionary efforts as soon as the obstacles which then existed had been removed. He claimed that these had now disappeared and called upon the Assembly to redeem its pledge. The motion was seconded by Principal Baird, another prominent member of the same party in the Church, and was carried *unanimously* and cordially.

The only echo of the former debate which could be detected in the speech of Dr. Inglis was the opinion which he volunteered that " little could be expected from mere preaching to an uneducated and barbarous people." This last remark called forth a strong protest which has been amply vindicated by the subsequent history of the Scottish Churches among such peoples in many fields.

It may be noted in passing that the view expressed by Dr. Inglis, the future Convener of the Foreign Missions of the Church of Scotland, was not without its influence on the determination of the line along which the first efforts of the first Mission of the Church of Scotland were directed, under the leadership of Dr. Alexander Duff.[1]

---

[1] The educational missionary work to which Dr. Duff mainly confined his efforts and the importance of which he never ceased to press upon the Church was not selected or devised by him ; but was from the beginning pursued in obedience to the specific instructions he had received when he set forth on his mission. " Of the plan," Dr. Duff himself said, " Dr. Inglis was the sole and undisputed author."   This is a point which has often been lost sight of in later discussions regarding this missionary policy.

H

The motion of Dr. Inglis asked the Assembly to appoint a Committee to report to the Assembly of 1825 and to lay before it a specific plan for the carrying out of the proposed missionary effort. This Committee was representative of both parties in the Church. Thus the missionary appeal brought for a time a happy unity into the Assembly of the Church.

The report of this Committee, which was presented to the Assembly in the following year (1825), recommended that the Church should begin its new enterprise by founding a Mission to India, the permission of the Directors of the East India Company having, it was stated, been obtained to entrance into India for this purpose. They suggested that a missionary collection be made throughout the Church *once in every five years*.

The year 1826 was a year of scarcity in in Scotland and the subscriptions received amounted to only £1240. An additional subscription, estimated at £90, was also promised. This disappointing result of their first attempt stirred the Committee to more energetic effort and the contributions received during the following year placed them in

a position to appoint a missionary. Alexander
Duff, who had just completed a distinguished
career at the University of St. Andrews, was
chosen to be their first missionary. Ordained
in August, 1829, Alexander Duff, after experiencing two shipwrecks in his voyage to
Calcutta round the Cape, reached his
destination in May, 1831, and began his
mission in the following July.

It is not proposed to enter into the history
of this Mission or of any of the other individual
Missions in India which owe their origin to
one or other of the Scottish Churches ; only
the important landmarks in the record of
Scotland's place in this early stage of its
modern missionary history need be given.
The Mission to Western India founded, as
has been already stated, by the Scottish
Missionary Society in 1823, continued under
the direction of that Society up to the year
1835. Of the seven pioneer missionaries
three now remained ; one had died, two had
to leave invalided, and one had become a
chaplain. The three who remained were
James Mitchell, in Poona, and Robert Nesbit
and John Wilson in Bombay. In 1835 these
missionaries petitioned the General Assembly

to be received as missionaries in connection
with the Foreign Mission Committee of the
Church. It was inevitable, now that the
Church had definitely entered the field of
Missions, that the Scottish Missionary Society
should disappear as a separate organization
and become absorbed into the wider organization of the Church of Scotland. It
accordingly agreed to the transference of its
missionaries and thus the oldest Scottish
Mission in India passed over to the Church.
The Mission which the Glasgow Missionary
Society had founded in South Africa was
similarly transferred, one part of it passing
over to the Church of Scotland, the other to
the Secession Church. In 1836 the Madras
Mission was founded by the Rev. John
Anderson as a Mission of the Church of
Scotland.

The last report before the Disruption, that
of 1842, records marked progress in the
Indian Mission. There were now thirteen
ordained missionaries and one unordained ;
three central stations—Bombay, Calcutta and
Madras—with many branch stations connected
with each of those centres, 2,000 scholars in
the schools of the Mission and several able

converts in training for the ministry. When
the Disruption took place all these missionaries declared their adhesion to the Free
Church of Scotland. Dr. Brunton, who had
succeeded Dr. Inglis in the Convenership,
had to face a great disaster to the work over
which he presided. In this crisis he bore
himself with a courage, a dignity and courtesy,
which won for him the high regard of all those
missionaries who had cast in their lot with the
Free Church. He had now to face the task
of reconstructing missions bereft of their
missionaries. Those missionaries, on the other
hand, had also to face the task of reconstruc-
tion especially in the matter of buildings.
The existing buildings remained in the
possession of the Church of Scotland ; con-
sequently new buildings had to be erected in
the various stations.

The enthusiasm which the Disruption had
called forth throughout Scotland and also
amongst Scotsmen in India enabled this to
be successfully accomplished. The Church of
Scotland also gradually succeeded in re-
equipping with missionaries its deserted
stations and thus for many years there were
two sets of Scottish Missions in the chief

centres.   There was this important difference
between the conditions created in Scotland
by the Disruption and those which resulted
from it in India, namely that in the mission
field there were few indications of rivalry and
hostility between the parties even from the
earliest stages of the great upheaval.   Losses
were patiently borne and made good without
recrimination.   The two sets of Scottish
Missions were enabled to keep " the unity
of the spirit in the bonds of peace."   The work
expanded through a separation that left no
bitterness behind it; and in the spacious fields
of heathenism there was ample room for both
sections of the Church of Scotland.   Antagon-
isms which within the narrow limits of
Scotland were often bitter found no root and
no nourishment in the soil of the mission
field.

Instead of these there grew up relationships
of brotherly co-operation which have now
become permanently established in centres in
which the work of the two branches of the
Church are under one united management.
Thus it is impossible to treat of Scotland's
missionary work in India without gathering
together into one comprehensive whole the

activities of the two Churches which in India
are already to all intents organically one.
While most Scotsmen are waiting with wistful
and impatient longing for the reunion of the
Scottish Churches the practical realization of
it has already been reached in the mission
field. It reached formal completion in the
Indian Church more than twenty years ago
when the Indian congregations connected
with seven separate Presbyterian Missions,
those of Scotland, England, Wales, Canada,
and the United States merged themselves
into one Church—the Presbyterian Church
in India.

The spiritual forces which have moved the
Churches in Scotland towards reunion may
be traced to their ultimate root in that
conception of the Christian Church which has
given birth in all the ages to missionary
enterprise and are due to the reaction on the
Home Churches of their work in world
evangelization. In the pursuit of a common
missionary ideal they have discovered their
essential oneness and are seeking to give to
it outward visible expression.

The same phenomenon is being witnessed in
other fields also, notably in Africa, where the

great missions, that of the United Free Church in Livingstonia and that of the Church of Scotland in the neighbouring field of Blantyre have taken a definite step in the same direction. In every field in which the Scottish Churches are at work this trend is visible.

CHAPTER VI

MORE than a century has passed since the Missionary Ideal regained a place in the thought and life of the Scottish Church. It seems therefore desirable at this point, in in order to form some idea of the stage which has now been reached, to take a comprehensive survey of the missionary efforts into which the Scottish Churches have been led in obedience to the new inspiration which then entered into their life. To trace in detail the development of the new movement through a century of missionary effort would be a task beyond the scope of the present discussion. Histories of individual missions are available for those who desire to pursue this minute study and in the numerous biographies of eminent missionaries additional abundant material has been provided. We content ourselves, therefore, with a brief picture exhibiting the wide field that is now covered by the missionary activities of the Scottish Churches and the immense variety of operation that is included in them.

(1) Without any attempt at chronological order let us survey in its geographical relations the far-flung line. In Europe and the nearer East the missionary operations of the Scottish Churches are mainly concerned with the Jewish nation distributed over several of the countries of Europe, chiefly in their great cities. In the Holy Land itself these churches have occupied a number of strategic points from which they are seeking to spread the Gospel of Jesus their Messiah among God's ancient people dwelling in their own land. Passing southwards to Arabia we reach the Scottish Mission to Muhammadans at Sheik-Othman on the outskirts of Aden, a Mission to the Arabs known as the Keith Falconer Mission, so named after its founder and first missionary, the son of the late Earl of Kintore. After a few brief years of labour this heroic missionary fell in the early prime of his manhood ; but the frontier post which he gained is still held. Travelling further eastwards we come to India, in nearly

every province of which we find the Scottish Churches at work. Beginning with Western India, the first district to be entered by Scottish missionaries, we follow a long line of Mission Stations of the Scottish Churches, Bombay and Poona, with numerous sub-stations attached to them, and as we advance eastwards we come upon the extensive rural Mission in the Dominions of the Nizam of Haidarabad with Jalna and the Christian village of Bethel near it, as the centre from which numerous villages in the surrounding territory are being evangelized. This Mission owes its foundations to the labours of two eminent Indian Christians, the Rev. Gunpatrao Navalkar and the Rev. Dr. Narayan Sheshadri, both converts from the higher castes of Hinduism, who were the fruit of the educational missionary work of the Free Church of Scotland in Bombay. Passing thence to the Central Provinces we find a Scottish Mission in Amravati, the capital of the Berar province and one of the great cotton centres in India, and again in Wardha and in Nagpur, the capital of the Central Provinces.

Nagpur is the principal centre of the

Scottish Mission in this part of India and connected with it are many sub-stations. Advancing further in the same eastward direction we come to Bengal and in the capital of India's most populous province we find a large representation of Scotland in this field. In Calcutta, with the numerous stations attached to it, Cninsurah, Khalna, and in the hill-country, Darjiling, Kurseong, Kalimpong, the Duárs and Sikkim, is found a great variety of missionary operations carried on by the two Scottish Churches. In Santhalia, also in the province of Bengal, there is a long established Mission to the aboriginal Santhal people, carried on from five missionary centres. Turning from the eastern to the north-western regions, we find in the Panjab a Scottish Mission at Gujrat, Sialkot, Wazirabad, Daska, Jalalpur and Jammu in Kashmir, where it borders on this part of the Panjab, these and several stations associated with them constituting one of the largest and most fruitful fields in the Indian Mission of the Church of Scotland. Coming to the South of India, we have most important Missions conducted by the Scottish Churches. These are found in

Madras, the capital of the Province, in Arconum, Chinglepat, Shriparambadur and Conjeveram, the great southern centre of Hinduism.

Returning to Central India we find in those territories, mostly under the direct rule of Indian Princes, which are included in the region known as Rajputana, an extensive chain of Mission stations, including Ajmere, Beawar, Nasirabad, Jaipur, Alwar, Jodhpur, Kotah, and Udaipur the most picturesque and romantic of them all, together with a number of stations the names of which are less familiar. This Mission in Rajputana was established by the United Presbyterian Church before its union with the Free Church of Scotland ; it drew to it some of the best life of that Church and sent back to it some of its best enthusiasms.

Pursuing our eastward route, we come to another great Empire, China. Here also we find extensive fields occupied by the Scottish Missions. The principal field is in Manchuria. Moukden and more than a dozen great and populous centres might be named ; but a mere enumeration of these would convey no adequate impression of the many-sided work which is being carried on there and the strong Chinese Christian Church which is springing out of it. Further south the Church of Scotland is carrying on a Chinese Mission which has its centre in Ichang, and still further south there is the Mission of the Presbyterian Church of England, which is to a large extent Scottish in as much as it has an auxiliary in Scotland and still draws a number of its missionaries from the ranks of the Scottish ministry.

We pass now to another hemisphere and another continent. Africa, in which Scottish missionary effort has been expended on a most extensive scale. It was Livingstone, a missionary from Scotland, who opened up the way into Darkest Africa. Scotland was already at work in the regions then known to the western nations before Livingstone awoke those enthusiasms that have drawn to Africa so many missions from so many Churches. Of these a very considerable proportion belong to the Scottish Churches.

To begin with the oldest, we find them in Kaffraria in the south and in Calabar on the west. Then when Livingstone's travels and

labours were ended, the heart of the Christian
Church went out to those regions associated
with his latest achievements.

The establishment of the Livingstonia
Mission on the shores of Lake Nyassa was
the first response from Scotland to the
challenge that came to Christendom from
Central Africa, through Livingstone's discoveries no longer a blank space on the map
of the continent of Africa, but a land teeming
with people of most virile tribes. For some
years the Livingstonia Mission had its own
separate organization ; but ultimately it
was absorbed into the general missionary
scheme of the Free Church of Scotland to
which most of its first missionaries belonged.
In the neighbouring district the Church of
Scotland founded the Blantyre Mission
working along similar lines. These two
Missions have created the Nyassaland
province now under British administration.
The " pax Britannica " now reigns among
races which not long ago knew nothing but
incessant inter-tribal war because to them
have been sent the messengers of the Gospel
of Peace.

Then during the War, the responsibilities

of the Scottish Churches in Africa were increased by the request addressed to them by the British Government to undertake the care of those mission fields from which Government was compelled by the exigencies of war to remove the German missionaries. Thus the German Mission in the Gold Coast and Togoland and the Moravian Mission in the Tanganjika region passed temporarily under their care. Now since the declaration of peace a number of those German missionaries have been permitted to return ; but it seems probable that the United Free Church will have to continue to hold part of the Gold Coast mission field as the Government will not permit the work to be carried on by German missionaries alone and insists on the continued presence of the Scottish missionaries in a certain proportion in a section of the field.

In East Africa also the Church of Scotland is at work in its Kikuyu Mission, the name of which came forward prominently in a great ecclesiastical controversy that arose a few years ago regarding intercommunion between the Anglican and other Churches.

In the province now known as Kenia,

there is also a Scottish Mission which is likely, under the new organization of this important province, to assume considerable proportions.

To complete the list of the portions of the world into which Scottish Missions have entered, there must be added those islands of the New Hebrides which were in the first instance evangelized from Scotland and are now a mission field of the daughter Presbyterian Church of Australia ; and the great island of Jamaica, one of the oldest missions of the United Presbyterian Church of the older days, which in its numerous self-supporting churches is a remarkable example of the blessing which follows persecution patiently endured and Christian labour persistently and successfully continued. It has been said of that great society which has taken the world for its province, the British and Foreign Bible Society, that the perusal of its annual reports is a liberal education. In like manner it may be said regarding this widespread activity of the Scottish Churches that no one can follow it as it pursues its ever-extending course around the globe without a vast widening of the horizon of his

I

intellectual interest and human sympathy. The cosmopolitan outlook for which Scotland is noted has been fostered not merely by the far-reaching commercial interests of its inhabitants, but also and perhaps in a manner more intense and more fruitful of benefit to the world, by its missionary enterprise. There can be little doubt that those members of the Scottish Church, who are in this intimate touch with the fields to which they have sent forth their missionaries in the service of Christ, have in numerous cases a more intelligent understanding of distant lands and nations than the majority of those who view the world simply from the standpoint of commerce or conquest.

(2) Consider this enterprise of these Scottish Churches as measured by financial standards.

When the Church of Scotland entered upon its missionary work, its first collection for missions made in 1826 amounted to £1,240. This sum was exceeded considerably in the following year ; but it still remained at a very modest figure. With this compare the figures of to-day.

From an early date in their history the

Foreign Mission in each of the Churches had an important auxiliary in the Women's Missionary Society, which raised funds specially destined for work among women and girls in the various fields. In the United Free Church the Foreign Missions Committee and the Committee of the Women's organization have already been amalgamated in the work of general Mission administration. In order to estimate correctly the progress made by the two Churches we must therefore include the income derived from this source in both Churches.

The total receipts in the two Churches from all these sources, including sums raised in the mission fields amounted in the year 1825, which marks the close of a century from the year in which the Church of Scotland resolved to enter upon missionary work, to £560,000. [1] Of this no less than a sum of £240,000 was contributed in the mission fields in the form of Government grants in aid of educational work, school and college fees, local subscriptions including £50,000 from the various native churches.

[1] Later figures show an increase under the various heads in this statement ; but it is convenient in this comparison to adhere to the figures of 1925.

This places the contributions of the Scottish Churches at £320,000. As has been noted, Government grants-in-aid and fees account for nearly £200,000 of the amount raised in the fields abroad. In India the Government grants and fees render the High Schools in many cases practically self-supporting, and in the case of the Colleges leave to be borne by the Church an expenditure which sometimes does not exceed a fourth of the whole. Thus in proportion to the extent of the work undertaken, and the influence which it is exerting on the nations which the Church is seeking to evangelize, its educational operations are the least expensive of its undertakings.

Looking for the present at the amount raised by the Churches, say, over £300,000, for the evangelization of the nations in that wide field which has been described, while we gratefully recognize the enormous advance which has been achieved, let us not for a moment imagine that Scotland has approached within measurable distance the ideal of Christian liberality to the cause of Missions which its earliest advocates set before them.

In the records of the Scottish Missionary Society will be found an appeal to Scottish Christians to set apart for the missionary cause a contribution of 1d. a week. It is scarcely credible, but it is true, that the Church's givings per member have not, after the lapse of more than a century reached that modest standard. When one thinks of the numberless ways in which this amount is being spent every day by almost everybody without a moment's thought, unnecessarily or for purposes that mean little for the well-being of ourselves or of others, one is amazed to see our great Churches struggling with deficits and utterly unable to respond to some of the most clamant needs of the mission field. But when we strike these averages we must not ignore those members of the Scottish Churches, who to the extent of their ability and with a splendid self-denial, have devoted themselves and much of their substance to the furthering of the missionary cause. In view of this, the only conclusion that can be drawn from the general result is that there must be a large proportion of the members of those Churches who do not give at all! A large section of the membership of the Churches still needs awakening and revival.

In these figures, however imposing in the aggregate they may appear, the Churches of Scotland can surely find little ground for self-complacency or self-congratulation and much reason for humiliation.

(3) To complete this survey let us turn to another set of figures more inspiring than those with which we have been dealing.

The number of missionaries, men and women in the mission fields of these Churches is approximately 750.

The number of native workers in the same fields is approximately 1,500, of whom 200 are pastors of congregations.

The total Christian community in all the Mission Churches associated with the Scottish Missions exceeds 300,000, increasing annually by about 10,000, i.e. by an annual increase of 3%. In India the percentage of increase in the Christian community is much in excess of that of the general population for the corresponding period. Of those 300,000, 120,000 are adults in full communion.

The scale on which the educational operations of these Missions are being carried on may be gathered from the following figures :

Number	of College students (in round figures)	. 3,700
,,	High School pupils	. 7,800
,,	Day Schools for boys and girls	. . 3,700
,,	Boys and girls in the above Schools	170,000
,,	Girls in the preceding total	. . 12,000
,,	Sunday School pupils	72,000

But statistics are, after all, not the most reliable test of missionary progress. It is heartening to those who rest not in supplication and effort for the spread of the kingdom of our Lord to know that in India, for example, the total number of Indian Christians of every name is now greater than the population of Scotland and that Christianity can now claim to be reckoned among the national religions of India, its adherents outnumbering the followers of at least two of the older religions of India, the Sikhs, and the Parsis, the followers of the Zoroastrian faith. But there is a more fundamental test than that of outward numerical growth. When we view, for instance, the problem of the Christianization of India in all its vastness, the question we ought to ask is not, How many converts to the Christian religion can be shown by the various Missions ? but, Has Christianity begun to lay hold of the Indian mind ? Has it struck its roots deep down into Indian soil ? Is it no longer a foreign importation but a religion that has become an Indian possession and capable of producing its own fruit in the land ? Has India assimilated it into its own life in a manner that gives promise of its permanence and its expansion from within ? It is only by such a process that the religion of Jesus can take possession of any people ; it is along lines like these that it has become the professed religion of all the nations that are now called Christian.

It is not to be denied that in the earlier stages of missionary endeavour sufficient care was not taken to prevent a certain measure of denationalization arising out of conversion to the Christian faith. In the case of savage races certain outward changes are inevitable and also desirable when the convert is brought by Christianity out of barbarism into a civilized life; but, even when in contact with nations of advanced civilization such as the peoples of India, missionaries were not always careful to discourage the tendency to imitate the ways of the West which was so apt to manifest itself among their converts. The adoption of European dress, of European names, was only too common among them. This kind of westernizing, which was by no means confined to Christian converts, but was in respect of dress spreading rapidly among those classes which had received a western education, is the least serious form in which it can manifest itself. When it shows itself in the imitation of western methods of religious and ecclesiastical expression that tend to cramp the free and natural expression of Indian Christianity through Indian channels, it is likely to imperil the growth and development of the Indian Church.[1]

---

[1] The attitude of Pandita Ramabai, whose work on behalf of Hindu widows has won for her a world-wide name, supplies an illustration of this tendency in what we might call its negative aspect, in her endeavour to abjure the use within the Christian religion of any words or names that have been associated in Hinduism with idolatry or superstition. She excludes the word *parameshvar* (supreme Lord) because in S. India it is a name of Siva, and even the word *putra* (son), the standing term in nearly

To-day this process of imitation has fallen into discredit and the policy of encouraging the free indigenous development of a faith, which claims a universal relation to the human race, has firmly established itself in all sound missionary plans. This is now the avowed policy of many modern missions and it is proclaimed by some as if it were a modern discovery. But as has been already stated in a previous chapter, it is no modern discovery ; but only the carrying out of an ideal which existed fully formed in the far-seeing minds of the great founders of Missions more than a century ago. Many of those modern discoveries prove to be only the recovery of something old which has been either lost or obscured in the interval. It has become almost an axiom to-day that Indian Christianity should wear an Indian garb and express its life in ways that reflect the temperament of those who have found in it the fulfilment of their

all the Sanskritic vernaculars of India for this relationship, because of a fictitious derivation of the word invented by the Brahmans after the doctrine of the son being the saviour of his father had been established. The derivation made the word mean " one who saves from Put," a hell, it would seem, invented for the purposes of this derivation as it plays no other part in Hindu mythology.

soul's highest quest. The fact that the Indian Church of to-day is claiming this form of spiritual independence is one of the most hopeful symptoms in the missionary experience of our time.

The awakening of a national consciousness among peoples from which it had long been absent is a conspicuous feature of the present time. This consciousness has been awakened in India and it is interesting to note that there it has arisen almost simultaneously in the political and in the religious sphere. One might be inclined to say that it shewed itself in the religious sphere before it found articulate expression in the political. This is what one might naturally expect, for the Christian doctrine of man prepares the way for the rise of this self-consciousness in the nation. It inculcates the principle of self-determination in the individual consciousness and there can never be a sound national consciousness that is not rooted in a deep sense of individual responsibility.

No doubt many other causes have co-operated in the creation of the situation that meets us to-day ; but the Christian contribution is undoubted. And it has shared also

in the result ; for the Indian Christian has
no desire to be detached from his non-
Christian countrymen and may be expected
to exert a healthful influence in any national
development in which he may be called to
play his part.

The Scottish Churches have met the
demands of the situation in a generous and
understanding spirit. They have welcomed
the desire that has arisen in the Indian Church
to be entrusted with new responsibilities
and have offered it an opportunity for
sharing with them the conduct of the work
in several fields. They recognize that
ultimately it must fall to the indigenous
Church to evangelize the millions of the land,
a task too vast for any foreign agency, and
that this is the method to which the history
of the Church of Christ clearly points. The
chief danger that attends the application
of this method is lest, in the initial stages
of the process, the indigenous Church should
lean too heavily on its foreign supports and
fail to realize the possibilities that may be
hidden in its own life. One cannot escape
the feeling that it would mean much more
for the indigenous Church to be entrusted

with a task all its own however humble it might be, to be carried out on its own initiative by its own resources and by its own self-denying labours, than simply to be granted a share in the management of a great enterprise initiated and supported mainly by the resources of a foreign Church. The Scottish Churches may yet discover that they can best encourage the indigenous Churches in their mission fields by directing them along the path of self-reliance and self-sacrifice along which they themselves have travelled from strength to strength. The method which has been attempted during the past two or three years has already revealed the danger to which reference has been made. In some mission fields the other method has been attempted and with far more encouraging result.

In addition to the advantages in such a method which have been already mentioned there are others which ought to commend its adoption. An indigenous Christian Church with its fuller knowledge of the genius of its people should be free to adopt those methods of evangelistic work which will make the most effective appeal to the thought and imagination of its own people, it can select its agency with greater knowledge and administer its own funds with wiser economy. There are already in India self-governing Churches and if these are to realize the missionary ideal of the Christian Church they must be encouraged to develop their missionary activities along lines of their own.

In view of the present condition of these Churches they may require in the initial stage assistance from the older Churches by which they have been planted, but those Churches in stimulating the missionary spirit of the indigenous Churches should not go beyond *assistance*. Accordingly some Missions have made the contribution by the indigenous Church of a tangible proportion of the expenditure involved a necessary condition of devolution. This condition is laid down with a definite expectation that the assistance in this form will diminish as the indigenous Church advances in this self-propagating effort. This is a truer form of devolution than simply to invite the newly formed Churches to share in the management of the work of a foreign Church which in its extent and costliness may be

utterly beyond its resources in money and
in workers in the present stage of its development.   In the light of what we may anticipate
from a system of devolution wisely directed,
the desire which has arisen in the indigenous
Churches to participate in aggressive
missionary work is one of the most hopeful
symptoms in the mission field.[1]

The outline which has been given of the
expanding Missions of the Scottish Churches
illustrates the working out of their revived
missionary ideal through a period of three
generations.   It is a record which is fitted
to inspire these Churches with thankfulness
and hope.   With the exception of the
Moravian Church which devotes seven-eighths
of its entire strength to specific missionary
work, most of it in inaccessible and difficult
fields into which it alone has ventured, few
Churches have made greater progress than
the Scottish Churches in their advance
towards the realization of the ideal which

---

[1] The mode of procedure that has been criticized is really due
to a certain devout imagination which sometimes mistakes its
own fervent desires for the actual fulfilment.   Those Churches
will grow into enterprise of this and of greater magnitude ; but
until they have reached a more advanced stage they cannot
bear the responsibilities that some would seek to lay upon them.
This will be discussed later in another connection.

is embedded in the true conception of the functions of the Christian Church. " Little among the thousands," Scotland has achieved much in the life of the world and the Scottish Churches have played no unimportant part as a spiritual influence throughout this process. Its very littleness may have led Scotland to seek those wider affinities ; but a truer explanation may be found in the temperament and spiritual make-up of the Scottish people which owes so much to its ancient Keltic inheritance. One would fain trace its large response, on the spiritual side, to the call of the world, to the missionary genius of those Keltic missionaries who first brought the light of the Gospel to its shores, and see in it the return to the Church of a later age of the spirit of the ancient Scottish Church, which made the little island of Iona to be not only the centre of a Christian Scotland, but also the focus from which the light spread through many lands through the perfervid apostles whom it sent forth. The prophecy of the dying saint of Iona with regard to his sacred isle is being fulfilled.

In the preceding chapter an attempt has been made to exhibit the extent and variety of the fields in which the Scottish Churches are conducting their missionary operations. In order to give a fuller understanding of what is included in this wide-spread effort of the Churches it is necessary to get nearer to it and examine in more detail the problems which they encounter and the methods by which they are endeavouring to solve them.

The fields are so varied that no single field includes within it all the types and degrees of civilization with which the Churches are confronted when they begin to obey their Lord's great commission to " go into all the world." The stages of civilization they meet with range from that of the untutored savage to that of cultured peoples which look back over periods of civilization that reckon their age in millenniums. In India we can find examples of most of the types referred to and from our experience of missionary conditions and methods in that richly variegated field we can gain instruction with regard to those to be found elsewhere.

While the goal of all missionary effort is one, the roads leading to it may be many and various. In one case it may mean the shaping of the language of a race that has no literature, in another the introduction of civilized means of living and supporting life, and in some the eradication of conceptions of God and His worship that rest on a philosophical tradition, subtle and profound, associated with names that have been revered through the centuries. This variety in mental, moral, and spiritual condition must make it evident that the way of approach to all cannot be the same. If the methods of the missionary Church are to be modelled on those of the Great Master they must adapt themselves to the special condition of the nations to which His message is being brought. One feature they must possess in common ; they must employ the only channel along which ennobling influence can pass from spirit to spirit, the channel of a Christ-like love.

Amongst the methods which are being followed in the fields that we have been contemplating the following are the chief : the simple proclamation of the Good Tidings in city-street or village market-place, by the roadside or in church, hall, or school, wherever the people can be gathered ; the work of healing carried on in mission dispensary or hospital or in the homes of the suffering ; educational work, whether carried on in the village school or in the city college or in the homes of the women in places where only thus can they be reached ; and also industrial training, indispensable in some cases if the Christian community is to develop along the lines of self-support and independence. All those types of operation are to be seen in the Scottish Mission field, as in the majority of the Missions at work in similar surroundings.

With regard to some of these no question has ever been raised within the Church. They lie so near to the lines of our Lord's ministry that they have been universally accepted as the standard methods of mission-ary work. But as missionary experience widened, it was soon discovered that many other activities, in addition to the simple proclamation of the Gospel, must be included in the work of the missionary. The missionary had to be not only a preacher, but also a healer, a teacher and a guide in many departments of the life of the people to whom he brought his spiritual message. This many-sided service has been nobly rendered and the transformation wrought by it in the lives of nations stands forth as one of the greatest miracles of the modern world.

For example, in many non-Christian lands the missionary had at the outset to minister to the sick and suffering even when his training for such a ministry was of the slenderest description. Thus at an early stage in missionary history the medical missionary, fully qualified and equipped was found to be indispensable in certain fields. The validity of this particular method has never been called in question, for the medical missionary was regarded as clearly following in the steps of the Master who went about doing good and healing all manner of diseases among the people.   Further, medical missions were found to be one of the most effective means for winning the trust and confidence of shy, suspicious and hostile tribes and of thus pioneering the way for the entrance of the Gospel into lands that seemed to be closed to every other method of approach.

The magic influence of the healer has been thus successfully employed by those who had no other motive than that of the exploring geographer or anthropologist. In a narrative of exploration published a year or two ago, Lady Richmond Brown tells us how she and her companion explorer in the Caribbean Sea and the adjoining continent so won the confidence of the people of the islands by the use of simple medicines which cured their ailments, that they were permitted to enter the territory occupied by an entirely unknown tribe into whose domain no one from the outside world had dared to penetrate, no member even of the native races that dwelt in the regions immediately adjoining the territory of those mysterious Indians.

But, while this is one of the results of the medical mission, it is not its ultimate source. To advocate the cause of medical missions on such grounds alone would be to ignore its higher, its real motive. The medical missionary does not exercise his healing art simply in order to win his way among the tribes. In healing the sick he feels that he is fulfilling a part of his Lord's commission. Jesus did not heal the sick in order to open a way for His message of the Kingdom. His works of healing were an integral part of His ministry and sprang from the same divine love that moved Him to give Himself in sacrificial life and sacrificial death for man's salvation.

When one sees a crowd of suffering men and women and children listening to the religious address which often precedes his medical ministrations, it may perhaps seem to those who are not in the secrets of the medical missionary's soul that this dispensary and hospital are being used simply to decoy these sufferers within the sound of the preacher's message. But the missionary knows that this is not the *raison d'être* of his mission. It stands on its own foundation as a Christ-work, attractive and effective by reason of the spirit in which the healing ministry is exercised. The Hospital is both historically and essentially a Christian institution. In the mission field it is the

Christian touch that draws the people to the Mission Hospital.

The point to be emphasized is that the medical missionary is a missionary when he heals, the nurse in the Mission Hospital is a missionary when she nurses, not simply when in spoken word they deliver their message. No other conception of his work would satisfy the medical missionary, no other inspire to such achievement as the men who have laboured in this spirit have reached. And no doubt has ever arisen in the mind of the Christian Church regarding the right of the Medical Mission to a place in its missionary programme.

When we pass to consider the educational missionary work of the Churches we approach a subject which unfortunately has been at various times surrounded by controversy. Its right to a place in the missionary programme has unfortunately been questioned. Although it has emerged successful in the discussions of the past, there are still so many individuals in the Churches, who still cherish misgivings, which, while they do not arrest the work, yet tend to limit the interest with which it is regarded in some quarters, that it is necessary to set this work in its proper light in the hope that those misgivings may be removed from the minds of some who are sincerely devoted to the missionary cause. This is specially necessary in any discussion of the Missionary problems of the Scottish Churches, for this is a department of missionary work in which they may be said to have specialized. In some of their fields, but especially in India, they have developed this form of missionary activity to such a point that, in addition to numerous vernacular schools and many High Schools imparting education in English, they maintain five Mission Colleges affiliated to the University of the Province in which they are situated. In these same provinces there are Schools and Colleges maintained by Government, and the question might very naturally suggest itself to the friends and supporters of Missions living in a country in which the State has assumed responsibility for the education of the people, Why should the Missions undertake work which lies within the sphere of the duties of Government ?

The answer to all such questions is furnished by the history of educational missionary work in India and by the conditions under which the Government of India is conducted, particularly the restrictions under which it is placed in any direct action in the sphere of education. This will be made clear by a brief reference to the circumstances under which the Churches were led to put their hand to this educational task.

When the Church of Scotland sent forth its first missionary, Alexander Duff, it instructed him to direct his efforts towards the imparting of a Christian education to the youth of India. As has been already stated in a previous chapter, Dr. Duff has explicitly disclaimed the credit of having originated this policy with which his name has been associated, ascribing it entirely to Dr. Inglis, the Convener of the Foreign Mission Committee of the Church of Scotland. In this he was no doubt guided by a very old Scottish tradition. John Knox had put his stamp upon it when he associated the work of the general education of the people with the Reformed Church, thus, unconsciously perhaps, reverting to the early ideals of the Keltic Scottish Church.

Alexander Duff arrived in Calcutta at what

medium of the English language. The Church
of Scotland has learned much since it first
put its hand to the work and to-day in some
parts of the Indian field its evangelistic
vernacular missions are the crown of its
labours. But in the earlier stages of its
work this method of spreading the Gospel
by preaching in the vernacular in the villages
and rural districts of India was not pressed
with the same energy that was thrown into
the educational effort. It was this want of
balance between the two sides of its work
that ultimately evoked the criticism to which
reference has been made. There is no
antagonism between these two methods of
evangelization ; they must go hand in hand
in all mission fields, and the final verdict
of those who appreciate the breadth of the
problem which the Church of Christ has to
face in the mission field will find its best
expression in the words : " These ought ye
to have done and not to leave the other
undone."

At the root of the criticism to which the
educational method has been subjected is
a profound misconception of its aim. The
existence of a similar misconception in

connection with medical missionary work
has been already noted. If this work were
carried on simply as an expedient for securing
an audience for the Gospel message it would
be difficult to justify the adoption of such
an elaborate and costly method of attracting
hearers and the medical work itself would
be shorn of its nobility. But, as we have
already shewn, the work of combating disease
and death amongst races over which disease
and suffering hold peculiar sway is in the
truest sense a Christ-like work, holding a
place in the mission of the Church similar
to that which it held in the mission of our
Lord. In like manner, to regard educational
work as simply an elaborate device for
bringing certain sections of the people of
India, China or Africa within reach of the
message of the Gospel—as a kind of bait
to draw them—would be to degrade this work
to a low level among Christian agencies.

Confining our thought, for the moment,
to India, although the argument is applicable
in substance to all mission fields, let us
endeavour to answer the question that is so
often asked : On what grounds is the Church
of Christ called to take the part which it

to utilize the work of the Missions in the field of education, began to treat it in the matter of its grants-in-aid with a niggardly hand. Out of the rivalry had come, at least in some parts of India, a scarcely masked hostility. The grievances which had arisen from the stepmotherly attitude which Government Educational Departments chose to assume in relation to aided education led to the appointment of an important Education Commission, the report of which, presented in 1883, speedily effected a marked change in the attitude of the Government to all forms of aided education. A forward movement in aided education soon followed. The beneficial changes that had been introduced still continue to operate. The Government no longer pursues a policy of discouragement in its relations with non-Government institutions ; but with impartial and generous hand aids it in its expanding growth. Only those who have worked through those two periods in the history of Indian education can know the full meaning of this change or appreciate the relief which it brought. Perhaps the portion of history that has now been recalled may explain, in part at least,

why the Churches of Scotland find themselves
to-day so deeply engaged in a great
educational work in India.

But behind this historical reason there is
the deeper ground which resides in the aim
of these colleges and schools to give to India
the kind of education that is necessary for the
real life of the people, an education which
the State is not in a position to offer, and
which constitutes a *preparatio evangelica* that
is spreading itself over the land.

Another period of struggle is imminent,
this time in relation to the maintenance of
this high aim. Under the reforms introduced into the Government of India by the
Act of Parliament of 1821, which has
transferred to legislative assemblies, a large
proportion of the members of which are
elected by the people, an extended jurisdiction,
the question of the unrestricted freedom in
religious teaching hitherto enjoyed by aided
educational institutions has now been raised
in a movement for the introduction of a
" conscience clause." No missionary would
hesitate in his decision regarding such a claim if
he were persuaded that compulsion was being
exercised in any matter of conscience. But,

L

quarters, among the enemies as well as among the friends of Missions, that education on a purely secular basis has failed to achieve what they alike desired—the moral uplift of the people. The demand for some means of moral instruction has been heard in all quarters and has given rise to much discussion among those who are sincerely concerned for the well-being of the people of India. The late Marquis of Dufferin, towards the close of his viceroyalty, in an important minute on this subject gave it as his opinion that the moral influence sought for could be best attained through institutions that imparted an education which was based on religion, and concluded by expressing the hope that such institutions might be greatly multiplied.

In view of the situation in regard to the matter of missionary education that has been created by the rise of a national consciousness both in India and in China, the Churches that are carrying on educational work in these great fields will be compelled to face the fundamental question as to their right to share in the education of the countries in which they have planted their Missions, and, especially in India, to make clear to themselves the conditions under which they can continue to play a part in the educational system of the land. They have entered this field in order to give to India the only kind of education in which they believe or which they are justified in offering, and as Churches they can only continue their educational agencies if they remain free to carry out their original purpose. On no other footing can the Scottish Churches consent to continue to share with the Government the task of educating the people of India. They cannot expect to retain the loyal support of their members unless they are untramelled, as they have been hitherto, on the religious side of their work.

But even when these conditions have been satisfied there will still remain those who cherish misgivings as to the value of this method of planting the Christian religion in India. It is often asserted that the visible result of the educational mission is, especially in more recent times, so insignificant in respect of the number of conversions to the Christian faith that the duty of the Churches to continue this form of work may be

Divine Spirit. But God does not carry out His wide purpose in this way alone. He often demands from His servants a faith, a patience and a hope which is content with the humble doing of His will with eye fixed upon Him, not on the immediate visible result. The glory of victory and triumph is not the inspiring motive of those who wait upon His word.

When the first impact of Christian teaching on the religious mind of India took place, the choice seemed to lie between the old traditional Hinduism with all its gross darkness and superstition, on the one hand, and Christianity on the other. For enlightened men there seemed to be no halting place between the two. But later a *via media*, or rather several *viæ mediæ*, came to be devised. " Reform and purify the old " became the cry, and societies, churches we might call them, sprang into being which sought to mediate between the higher light shed by Christianity, from which came the impulse to seek a purer faith, and the religion which, in the form in which it had been inherited, was no longer possible. The *samaj* or religious society was a refuge for

many, and numbers of high-souled earnest
thinkers found a resting place there. These
spoke with a Christian accent ; they adopted
many Christian ideals ; and while they
reverenced Christ almost to the point of
worship, and sought to adopt His teaching as
containing the highest standard of human
conduct, they had no place for Him as a
Divine Saviour nor for His cross as the
expression of redeeming love. Not only did
such *samaj's* come into being, but also a new
interpretation of Hinduism came into vogue.
The things in Hinduism which revolted the
enlightened conscience were explained and
explained away. The uncultured, it began
to be said, might need idols in their worship
and be helped by them to the realization of
the Divine Presence ; but the higher minds
had no use for such gross forms of worship
and if, for reasons connected with the preservation of caste and social standing, they
might on occasion join in such outward
worship, inwardly they felt themselves to be
independent of such external aids, which to
them were merely symbols of a spiritual
reality which they were able to apprehend
without them.

had been gathered into the Church of Christ mainly through mission schools. He held, at the same time, that our duty as missionaries was not to be measured by results in any department of our work. Referring to his own special work, evangelistic work carried on mainly by preaching in the streets and open spaces of the city of Bombay, he added that, although he could not trace a single conversion to the street-preaching in which for years he had been engaged, he would continue to preach in the streets of the city to the end of his life. And he did.

The inadequacy of the merely statistical test in relation to particular forms of work has been insisted upon. But one may say that what has been insisted upon in this connection is really applicable to all forms of missionary activity. There are great mass movements in the mission fields to-day, They are a ground for profound gratitude to God and for increasing hopeful effort on the part of the Churches. This does not arise simply from the reported statistics of numerous baptisms ; but from the increasing number of people who are being thus brought within the sphere of Christian effort. This large ingathering is laying the foundation of a Christian community ; but every Christian worker in such fields knows that it is after baptism that the real evangelistic work has to be carried out. This is a slower process, but by such processes the spiritual temple is being reared, and to the completeness of the structure every type of work done in the Saviour's name and in His spirit is bringing its contribution.

UP to this point we have been considering the Missionary Ideal in its action upon the non-Christian world. We must now change our point of view and ask, In what manner and to what extent has this missionary activity on the part of the Churches re-acted on their thought and life ? This interesting inquiry naturally divides itself into two parts, one dealing with the thought and the other with the life of the missionary Church. These will form the subject of this and the following chapter.

When one looks back over the Christian centuries one cannot fail to discern the influence of historical environment on the form in which Christian theology has defined its position in regard to the central problems of the Christian faith. The fact that it has shewn itself to be capable of such a response to an environment of thought that has passed through so many phases is indeed one of the most striking proofs of its essential vitality. In this respect it bears the stamp of every living thing.

In its ancient creeds we find Christian thought expressing itself in terms of the mental categories of the time, and every succeeding era has exhibited the same phenomenon. It is also found that the periods which give birth to these formulations of Christ-doctrine in creeds and confessions have had one feature in common ; they have been marked by some great religious movement out of which have emerged those historical symbols of the Church's faith. In our own age there has arisen a demand both in the Churches of Scotland and in the Church of England for a statement of the faith of the Church suited to the environment of the thought of the present age. Whatever views may be held as to the capacity of our time for real achievement, one thing is certain, namely, that no such attempt can hope to be successful that is not borne on the wave of a great spiritual movement. The urge must come

not simply from a merely intellectual need ;
it must spring out of a profound stirring of
the spiritual life of the Church.   There is one
direction to which the signs of the times seem
to be pointing as that from which such movements might be expected to arise.   For
simultaneously with the widespread awakening of a national consciousness among the
peoples of the world there has also arisen a
wider view of international responsibility.
Throughout the world people are thinking in
wider terms, and in like manner the Churches
also are awakening to the consciousness that
their field is the world.   The future of the
Christian Church is largely bound up with
the response which it will make to this wider
outlook.

Many can still remember the keenness with
which years ago the question was debated
as to whether any race or tribe had been
discovered which was absolutely destitute
of a religious consciousness and anything
that might be regarded as religious worship.
Some travellers had reported the discovery
of such peoples ; but many were disposed to
doubt the accuracy of their reports and the
impartiality as well as the capacity of the

witnesses. To-day it is the generally
accepted opinion that no such race has yet
been found, that humanity, even on its
lowest plane, manifests a consciousness of a
relation to some higher power outside and
above itself ; but one wonders why this
controversy excited so much warmth of
debate in both theological and anti-theo-
logical circles, seeing that its determination
in one way or the other does not affect the
validity of religious experience wherever it
is found. Any race found to be destitute of
a religious sense would be found also dis-
qualified for classification in the ranks of
humanity.

The interest awakened by this inquiry was,
however, preparing the way for the emergence
of a new branch of study now extensively
pursued under the name of the Science of
Comparative Religion. In the evolution of
this modern science two opposite extremes
have manifested themselves, one in its
earliest, the other in its latest development.
The former is represented by those theologians who thought to confirm the authority
of the Christian Scriptures by shewing that
parallels to the facts which they record

M

could be found in the non-Christian religious
books which must have borrowed these from
the Bible narrative or derived them from the
same common source.   Even so distinguished
an Oriental scholar as Sir William Jones was
entrapped by an effort made to establish
this position.   A contemporary of this
scholar [1] made an attempt to find out from
the Brahman pundits whether they had any
parallels in their Shastras to the Old Testament stories which he related to them.   He
offered ample rewards for any extracts from
their sacred books that might be produced to
him containing stories parallel to that of
Adam and Eve in the Christian Scriptures
and those of Deukalion and Prometheus in
the Mythology of Greece, etc.   The rewards
offered produced in time a copious supply ;
but it was subsequently discovered that the
astute pundits had themselves translated the
various stories that had been recited to them
into Sanskṛit, their sacred language, and had
inserted leaves containing those fabrications
of their own making into the body of some
of the MS. copies of their Sacred Texts.

[1] Lieutenant Wilford.   Cf, Max Müller's *Selected Essays*,
Vol. II, pp. 451-2.

These fabricated coincidences were indeed so numerous that the suspicion of fraud was soon awakened ; they were too good to be true. The fraud was publicly exposed ; but not before these faked scriptures had been read all over Europe and had deceived many.

Among modern representatives of this science are some who aim at reducing all religions, including Christianity, to the same naturalistic origin, the implication being that Christianity has its place along with other religions in the ascending scale of religious evolution. This has created in some Christian minds a prejudice against the entire branch of study that is included under the name of Comparative Religion. In his recent work, entitled *The Everlasting Man*, Mr. G. K. Chesterton has given forceful expression to this feeling. He protests against the idea that the Christian religion can be included in such a comparison of religions, seeing that it is unique in character and origin and cannot be studied in the same category with the ethnic faiths. This is a perfectly valid protest as against the method in which this subject has been treated by many investigators, and one which will be endorsed also

by Christian theologians whose standpoint
is different from that of this writer who
speaks as a member of the Roman Catholic
Church. But, even when the fullest regard
is had to the considerations advanced in
this protest against the methods which have
been pursued, there remains a wide and an
attractive field for the study of religion by
tracing the various forms in which it has
manifested itself in the various nations of the
world throughout the course of human
history. Such a study has also its contributions to offer to the Christian Church in
the enrichment and deepening of its theological conceptions. The advance of those
" comparative " studies owes much to
Christian missionaries whose intimate knowledge of the peoples concerned in those
inquiries has enabled them to interpret to
others the religious conceptions and aspirations of the followers of ancient faiths.

A true appreciation of what lies beneath
those age-long strivings after God has effected
a change in the mode of the missionary
approach to the non-Christian mind. Just
as in the early age of the Christian Church
its attitude toward the non-Christian world

presents changing aspects, so in the modern
age similar changes may be observed in the
attitude of the Church toward the faiths of
the peoples with which it has a missionary
contact. Among the Early Fathers there
were some whose attitude seems to have
been one of uncompromising hostility. These
saw in the virtues of the heathen world only
" splendid (shining) vices." But there were
other Christian Fathers who, with a pro-
founder and more sympathetic insight, saw
in them the fruits of a divine influence
proceeding from the Eternal Christ. They
saw the Spirit of Christ at work in the hearts
of men to whom the message of the Cross
had not yet come. Such an one was Justin
Martyr and such also was Clement of Alex-
andria, himself an example of the brooding
of the Divine Spirit over the darkness of the
heathen world. And in our own time the
wider knowledge, that has come to us of the
nations through the intimate contact of
missionaries with some of the noblest spirits
among non-Christian peoples, has deepened
in many the conviction that the action of the
" Logos " has not been confined to those
whose hands touched the Word made flesh

or those to whom their witness came. Those of us who have come into intimate contact, for example, with some of the purer spirits to be met with in the very heart of Hinduism are compelled to believe that God does work in the souls of men in ways which we cannot trace or explain.[1]

From such sporadic phenomena to proceed however to the conclusion that those religions had in them the seed of a higher development which reached its fulfilment, when the Word was manifested in the flesh with the advent of Jesus Christ, is a step which finds no warrant either in apostolic teaching or in the historical development of non-Christian religions. The tendency towards a rash generalization of this nature is occasionally to be met with in some of the missionary literature of our time. There is an illustration of this in a work entitled *The Crown of Hinduism* published not many years ago

---

[1] The writer recalls one of those who long before he had seen a Christian missionary or had in any way, directly or indirectly, been influenced by Christian teaching passed unscathed through temptations of the fiercest and most dangerous nature and emerged with conscience undefiled. Can experiences like this be traced to the religious atmosphere in which such exceptional men have been reared, or must we not rather ascribe them to the work of the divine *Logos* immanent in lives which stand out so luminous against the general darkness ?

by a writer who has rendered great service both as a missionary and as a sympathetic student of modern religious movements in India, especially within Hinduism. This work contains much that is valuable and instructive in regard to that background of longing and aspiration which stands behind so many of the phases of Hindu religious belief and practice ; but when the meaning of the title unfolds itself and one finds that Christianity is the crown of the development pictured in this work one feels that the facts are being strained to support a foregone conclusion which they of themselves do not warrant. This writer seems to find in Hinduism the seed-ground of Christian ideals and in Christianity the goal towards which Hinduism has been leading. This is no doubt an alluring picture ; it has fascinated the mind of the author and probably also the minds of many of his readers. But when his zeal for the fullest illustration of his position leads him to find in " sati," the terrible rite in which the Hindu widow immolates herself on the funeral pyre of her husband, an adumbration, of some sort, of a Christian ideal, that of self-sacrifice, those who are eager to

welcome every element of good that they can
discover in every non-Christian faith, must
refuse to follow him along this dangerous
path. Christianity is not the crown of
Hinduism or of any of the ethnic religions of
the world.

The missionaries of the Cross in apostolic
days had just as good reason to regard the
religion which they proclaimed as the crown
of the pagan religions of Greece and Rome
which were not lacking in things of artistic
and moral beauty. To these the apostles
were not blind nor to the evidences of
spiritual aspiration which they revealed;
but their interpretation of the relation which
they bore to the religion of Christ was very
different from that which has been under
discussion. Witness the line of approach
which St. Paul chose in addressing an
Athenian audience. It may well be taken as
our model. With wondrous tact he
commends the Athenians for the place which
they gave to religion in their thought and
practice. In the inscription " To the Unknown God " which he had read on one of
their altars he sees their scrupulous anxiety
that no divine being should be left out of

their worship ; he is touched by their
religiousness (it is unfortunate that the
word " superstitious " of the A.V. has so
long obscured the true sense of the apostle's
words) and with sympathetic hand he guides
them towards the knowledge of the God
whom they are worshipping all unknowing.
This God is One who is not to be found in
such objects of worship as they have devised,
but a God who is the Father of us all and
cannot therefore be embodied in the gold or
silver or stone graven by art and man's
device.   Yet while he thus declares the
failure of their search after God he vindicates
the search itself as included in the divine
purpose.   They have not been left out of that
purpose of God ; the time of its fulfilment has
come.   And when Paul writes to the Greeks
of Corinth he declares to them also the failure
of human wisdom, he tells them of the same
purpose of God and of its gracious fulfilment
in Jesus Christ.   " When in the wisdom of
God the world by wisdom knew not God it
pleased God by the foolishness of preaching
to save them that believe."

The saying of Jesus " I am not come to
destroy but to fulfil " is often loosely quoted

in support of the view that those ethnic
religions represent stages of development
that find their culmination in Christianity.
If it be interpreted in the sense that those
strivings after the knowledge of God find
their fulfilment in the revelation of Jesus
Christ, this application of the words of our
Lord is in full accord with the teaching of
the apostles ; but if it is quoted in support of
the view that Christianity is the fulfilment of
those religions in which man's search after
God found expression, this form of interpretation is without warrant. It ignores the
context in which the saying of our Lord was
uttered. The words will not bear this wide
application. Jesus when He spoke these
words was unfolding to His hearers the
spiritual content of the Mosaic Law. He
had condemned the formalities which had
gathered round its interpretation and had
quenched its life. His words of condemnation might have seemed to his enemies hostile
and destructive. He therefore tells them
that He is not destroying but fulfiling their
Law. There are many cases in which the
words of our Lord are pregnant with wide
and far-reaching applications, but this is clearly

not one of those. If the religion of Jesus be the fulfilment, the culmination of a process of development in which all other religions are to be regarded as preliminary stages, will the nations which cling so tenaciously to their ancient faiths be ready to relax their grasp of them on the invitation of a religion coming from without that claims simply to be the consummation or crown of their own? Will they not rather ask, as some of them are asking to-day, to be allowed to work out this consummation for themselves?

But while this overstrained conception of an organic relation of Christianity to those religions must be discarded are we to regard them as standing in no relation to Christianity? Have they no important place in the preparation of the way of the Lord? In a different sense from the above they do stand in a most vital relation to the dispensation of the Gospel of Christ. What are they but the stretching forth of the human spirit towards God in all the various ways in which they have sought to apprehend Him, whether as an unseen mysterious Power dominating the life of His creatures through physical agencies, which man personifies into gods to be worshipped, or as an all-pervading spirit dwelling in every created thing, including man himself, or as in the highest range of their aspiration they had glimpses of him as the divine Father of all ?

> "Like plants in mines which never saw the sun,
>   But dream of him, and guess where he may be
>   And do their best to climb and get to him."

This Godward impulse is of God's own creation and in Jesus Christ His Son He graciously draws near to meet it. This striving after God is the growing revelation of a human need which is, in the truest sense, a preparation of the way of the Lord. It is found not only in the religious writers, especially the poets, who from time to time have arisen among those peoples to give voice to their aspirations, but also in a manner no less impressive in their constant religious practice. In that part of India in which the writer has spent long years there has been a remarkable succession of poets who are known as " the saints of Maharashtra." Their poems are almost exclusively religious, and some of them continue to be the nourishers of the piety of the nation. No one can read these without being arrested by their earnest devotional spirit and the deep discernment which they reveal of the real need of the soul in its striving after God. One feels that some of the passages in these poems, if separated from their context which is still resonant with the sounds of the idolatry in which the writers were still rooted, might almost take a place alongside the Psalms of the Old Testament, of which they would almost seem to be an echo. One reads them with a thrill of emotion which draws the heart in longing sympathy to the people to whom such glimpses of the higher vision were vouchsafed. Nothing in literature can touch one more than the springing up of such beauteous flowers out of a soil otherwise cumbered with many noxious growths. The Spirit of God has indeed been brooding over many regions of our world and there has been some response to His upward drawing. These nations have not lain outside the purpose of God as it moved forward to the fulness of the times.

Impressive also is the testimony which is borne by the daily religious practice of these flow to the enrichment of Christian faith and experience.

Think of the significance of this God-consciousness of India. Spinoza would have called India a " God-intoxicated " land. Behind and beneath the idol-worship and all the degrading customs that are associated with it there is a consciousness of the presence of God in the world of men and things which is not the result of the inferences of thought but an immediate experience. To the Indian who thinks philosophically, God is the ultimate, the only reality ; in the case of the ordinary man the consciousness of God has sunk so deeply into his life that religion, at least in the form of outward ceremony, has come to be associated with its commonest acts. Does not this shew traces of an ideal that spiritually realized might become capable of the noblest uses ? On the foundation of such an underlying consciousness Christianity as a spiritual transforming force can rear a structure of true spiritual beauty. We do not want the formalism of mechanical rite and ceremony to which its expression has degenerated in the religious life of the multi-tudes ; but we do want the spirit out of which it has sprung. And who will say that we do not need it? Is it not one of the great defects of those habits of mind into which we have grown that we too often fail to connect God with the ordinary affairs of our daily life, that our God-consciousness is so fitful and so largely confined to special times of devotion and worship? As an experience, existing by itself apart from our intellectual and moral consciousness, the realization of the presence of God may not achieve much that is fruitful or abiding, but when it permeates life in the entirety of its thought and action it reaches a true consummation.

Long ages of concentrated feeling after God have left to the Indian the inheritance of a mind in which have been prepared the channels along which such an experience may flow.

And those who have any real acquaintance with Indian Christianity, as seen in converts to the faith who have had a real spiritual experience, can bear testimony to the influence of the attitude of mind which has been above described on Indian Christian piety. Every one who has studied the Indian conception of union with God must be aware of

N

of a higher use. The thought of the transcendence of God over all His works which it was the special function of the Old Testament revelation to proclaim and preserve was lost to India when its religious development came under the dominance of abstract speculation which ended in the elimination of personality in respect both of God and of man. A system of thought which aimed at a logical completeness and failed to take account of the moral foundations of man's personality, as these were glimpsed in the ancient Aryan thought of man's relation to the divine order, became one-sided and ended in the most thorough-going pantheism which the human mind has reached. Yet the thought of the immanence of God in creation is one for which the Christian religion has a legitimate place, without which some of its deepest truths cannot be apprehended in their full significance.

In the Gospel according to St. John the idea of the indwelling presence of God is unfolded in the doctrine both of the incarnation of God in Jesus "the Word Who was in the beginning with God" and also of the indwelling of Jesus in His disciples. When

God, the Creator, Who stands in His transcendence above all His works, became incarnate and dwelt among men in the person of His Son the transcendence and the immanence of God were revealed in their complete synthesis in the Christ Who is the "express image of His person." "This," says St. John, "is the true (the real) God." The idea of Incarnation lies very near to the common lines of Hindu thought as is seen in the "avatárs" which occupy such a prominent place in Hindu mythology. To the Hindu mind the idea of the incarnation of God in Jesus Christ presents no initial difficulty as it does to the Muhammadan whose particular form of theistic belief tends to the isolation of God from Creation as an irresistible almighty power working upon it without drawing near to it.

Similarly, our Lord's teaching regarding His relation to His own is expressed in the language of immanence. He sums it up in the words addressed to His disciples—"Abide in me and I in you." Must not then that habit of mind to which our attention has now been drawn make it easier for those who have inherited it to assimilate the Christian

conception of God's relation to man as revealed in the Son and of the indwelling of this
Divine Redeemer in the lives of those who are
united to Him in faith and love ?

When in the writings of certain schools
of Hindu religion we meet poetic language
that seems to approach this form of high
spiritual experience, should we not recognize
that to those earnest souls who were seeking
God was vouchsafed a glimpse of the path
along which He would be found ?

There is another feature of our Christian
life which receives reinforcement from the
traditionary conceptions of the nature of
religion that are met with in certain non-
Christian faiths. We refer to the sense of
solidarity, the consciousness of the fact of a
corporate life among its members which is
so fundamental to the well-being of the
Church of Christ.

This sense of solidarity is most conspicuous
in the religion of Islam and is seen also in
many of the religions of the East. This is,
for example, the secret of the success of Islam
in winning those African tribes amongst
which, we are told, its propaganda is being
strenuously pushed. The convert to Islam,

by whatever path he has been led to embrace
this faith, finds himself to have become at
once a member of a great brotherhood.
Race distinctions have become obliterated.
The negro who has learned to repeat the
brief confession of Islamic faith finds himself
admitted to fellowship and brotherhood by
his Aryan co-religionists of every shade of
colour.   The limited ethical demand which
Islam makes on these untutored races and
the prospect which it secures for them of
admission to this wide brotherhood are
amongst the chief influences that help forward those Islamic movements.   The choice
between Islam and the sword is no longer
now the alternative that is offered.

Divided up into many sections, separated
from each other by the impassable barriers
of caste, even Hinduism exhibits, within each
individual caste, this sense of solidarity in
its intensest form.   There the communal
sense has reached its perfect development.
The individual has been almost lost.   He has
become simply a part of a great system in
which he is incorporated, his action is dictated
by the common will and his standard of right
is simply the accepted custom of the caste.

Now the experience of the Churches that are at work in the mission field offers them many illustrations of this solidarity of life as an essential feature of the Christian religion. For this consciousness of membership in one body is an outstanding feature of those communities of Christians, that have been formed as the result of their labours, in non-Christian lands. Even caste-feeling, that hardest to eradicate of all anti-social feelings, is being eliminated from the body of the Christian Church. The Brahman and the outcast are being merged into the same consolidated life. The feeling common to all the religions from which converts have been gathered, that religion is the strongest bond of human fellowship, has made the response to the Christian demand less difficult. It is one of the most remarkable features in the relation of the Hindu to the Christian convert that while the Hindu may regard the outcast as " untouchable " he seems to regard the outcast convert to Christianity as belonging to another category. The enlightened Hindu admits him to a measure of social intercourse which he would have denied him if he had remained an outcast in his old community.   He regards him now as a member of a new brotherhood, distinct from that of the caste to which he himself belongs, but no longer entitled to his contempt.

And within the Christian community there is among the various sections of the Christian Church a drawing towards each other as followers of the same faith, which goes far beyond anything of the same nature to be found in the older Churches of the West. This may be due in part to the position in which they stand, surrounded by so many religious communities different in religious faith and hostile to their own; but it is largely the result of that communal sense which is so imprinted on the Indian mind.   They are closing their ranks and are moving toward an outward unity at a much more rapid rate than the Churches of the West.   It may safely be asserted, because it is profoundly true, that if those influences which keep them apart, namely, those due to the accident of their original connection with the particular section of the Western Church to which they owe their conversion, were removed, the Indian Christians would speedily coalesce into one and constitute themselves an Indian

Christian Church ordered and governed in accordance with their own national genius, as the far-seeing founders of the modern Mission contemplated when they led the Church out to its world-wide task. No doubt there would be in the East, as has been found in the West, exceptions to this general movement. Wherever high sacramentarian conceptions regarding the Church and its ministry are dominant difficulties will be encountered ; but what has been stated is still true in regard to the great body of evangelical Christianity in the land.

In Scotland we are facing this problem now, so far as the Presbyterian Churches are concerned. In India a much more comprehensive union has long ago been achieved. Practically all the Churches connected with the Presbyterian Missions have been merged in one. A further advance has been made in this uniting process. There is now a South Indian Church in which all these have united with the Congregational Churches, and more recently the Church of North India has widened its constitution to include the same section of the Church in that area. And the process of increasing union will go on.

Here again we see that the solution of the problems of the Churches at home is to be found not by looking inwards, but by looking outwards beyond themselves at the need of the wider world. To build Jerusalem in Scotland's green and pleasant land, what is needed is a great missionary enthusiasm, a revival of that consciousness of a mission to the world that has been a feature of the life of the Scottish Churches in all the best and most fruitful periods of their history from its first beginning. Of the Church as of the individual is this saying true, that it must die that it may live, die to the thought of itself as an end that it may live to the wider purpose of the Kingdom of God.

AMONG the many criticisms that are directed against the Church to-day none is more serious than that which is embodied in the complaint so often heard that it has lost the accent of confidence and assurance that was so characteristic of its message in apostolic days. When St. Paul, during his Corinthian Mission, gazed across the waters that separated him from the Italian shores, with his face and his desire turned towards the imperial city, it would seem that for a moment he felt a touch of the misgiving that the vision of Rome as the centre of the world's power was fitted to awaken. But this misgiving is no sooner awakened than it is brushed aside ; the faith of the apostle rises triumphant over every doubt in the challenging word—" I am not ashamed of the Gospel of Christ, for it is the power of God."

His confidence in the power of the Gospel was based on a two-fold experience. The memory of that vision of the ascended Lord, which flashed upon him on the Damascus way and made the Gospel of Christ the power of God to him, was ever with him. And as he carried the message of this Gospel from city to city, from country to country, his sense of its power gained added strength. In the city of Corinth, in which he had laboured for many days, he had witnessed new and convincing demonstrations of this power. Out of the darkest depths of heathenism in the most polluted centre of the vice and ungodliness of that age he had seen many pass into into the marvellous light of Christ. Over against the hopelessness of the wisdom of the world stood forth the power of the Gospel to save and to restore.

These two sources of confidence are available for the Church to-day. They are indeed so closely bound together that the one is absolutely necessary to the other. The Church that is able to say, "I am not ashamed," must draw its confidence from both. It

is presented to us in the teaching of our Lord and His apostles ! This is seen in the multitudinous details of our common life ; it is quite as conspicuous in the indifference, which is manifested by so many who profess and call themselves Christians, to the supreme motive of our Saviour's humiliation and passion.   All this is the result of substituting the Church, its observances and the conventional standards of Christian life which find shelter within it, for the Kingdom of God which Jesus came to establish in the world. What the Church needs, and even the world is asking for it, is *reality*, a larger measure of sincerity in its profession and its life.   Mere emotion is not enough ; unless this emotion finds expression otherwise than merely in speech or song it profiteth nothing.   When in the worship of the great congregation we join in singing with high emotion the words of consecration which the survey of the wondrous cross called forth from the soul of the poet :

> " Love so amazing, so divine,
>   Demands my soul, my life, my all,"

how many of us realize the full meaning of

our adoring praise ? What would it not mean for the Church of Christ if those of us who worship the Saviour in words of such lofty devotion, inspired by the vision of His cross, were ready to respond to the appeal of our crucified Lord. The Scottish Churches to-day are calling for the service of consecrated men and women to fill vacant places in many fields, for the means to send them, and one hears to-day the ominous word " retrench-ment " in connection with a work in which the retreat signal dare not be sounded. Should such things be possible among those who have pledged to the service of their Lord " soul, life and all " ?

Let us now view the situation from the other side and consider the influence of the missionary ideal on the reviving and quick-ening of the life of the Church.

The Church of Christ has always had, even in its darkest ages, men and women devoted and saintly, who even in the midst of most unfavourable surroundings were moved by the love of their Saviour to listen to the call that came to them from the darkness of the heathen world. To such we owe the inception, at various periods, of missionary enterprise

o

within the Churches to which they belonged. The outward movement which they inaugurated proved also to be the beginning of a new life within the Church. Scotland was no exception to this general experience ; it owes more than it knows to the reaction of such missionary endeavour on the evangelical life of its people. Those who were the leaders of those movements kept in close touch with the work which they had initiated, and by keeping themselves and their people informed regarding its progress helped to raise their Churches to a higher spiritual level. The piety of the Scottish Church in those days was largely nourished on the food supplied to them in the missionary literature of the early years of last century. The same influence is still and on a larger scale at work to-day in the Scottish Churches. Let us indicate briefly some of the lines along which this influence is working.

It has, in the first instance, confirmed and strengthened the confidence of the Church in the message with which it has been entrusted. The history of modern missions has exhibited to the Church evidences of the divine power of the Gospel of Christ as striking and as